Delna Prakashan

WHIP IT!

This edition was published by The Dreamwork Collective
The Dreamwork Collective LLC, Dubai, United Arab Emirates
thedreamworkcollective.com

Printed and bound in the United Arab Emirates
Food Photography: Barry Morgan
Food Styling: Henriett Braun
Book Design: Myriam Arab

Copyright © Delna Prakashan, 2019

ISBN 9789948364672

Approved by National Media Council
Dubai, United Arab Emirates
Approval number: MC-02-01-9313818
Printed and bound in the United Arab Emirates
by Al Ghurair Printing and Publishing LLC

♻ Printed using 100% recycled paper

Delna Prakashan

WHIP IT!

A GUIDE TO GETTING

SASSY & SKILLED

IN THE KITCHEN

THE
DREAMWORK
COLLECTIVE

DEDICATION

To my mom.

We squabble, we share, we explore.

Thank you for teaching me about life during our many conversations in the kitchen and over meals.

You will always be my rock, my north star, my best friend.

—

EAT LIKE A KID, VISIT NEW PLACES, EXPLORE CULTURES...

THE WORLD'S FILLED WITH FINGER-LICKIN' SMACKALICIOUS AWESOME FOOD THAT'S TOO DAMN GOOD TO BE MISSED!

—

TABLE
OF CONTENTS

- INTRODUCTION · 07
- THE HOW-TO GUIDE TO GETTING SASSY AND SKILLED · 17
- BREAKFAST QUICKIES · 37
- LUNCH OR NOT TO LUNCH? · 61
- BEFORE DINNER MUNCHIES · 89
- EASY-PEASY-LEMON-SQUEEZY DINNERS · 113
- THIS ONE IS A KEEPER · 145
- SWEET ENDINGS · 151
- HOST YOUR PARTY LIKE A PRO · 169
- RECIPES FOR WHEN... · 182

If you're like me and the day kick-starts with a list of to-dos and events to look forward to, you'll recognise that sweet kind of anxiousness creeping in.

You want to give it all your best and breeze through the day, but there's just *so much* to do. Top that with the idea of spending time in the kitchen, and cooking can then feel like just another chore to tick off. Besides, with the number of delivery apps and take-out options available, why struggle anyway? Right?

But wait. What if I told you there's a way to turn this 'chore' of cooking to one of the best parts of your day? That the kitchen is not just about cooking a meal for yourself, it's also a place where you decompress and reflect?

You *can* whip up a meal while also relaxing and having fun. **IT'S POSSIBLE—I PROMISE.**

But I hear you and know what that mumble-jumble of thoughts can feel like. Here's a sneak-peak of a typical day in my life…

8.00 p.m.

I've just left the office.

Oops, just remembered I need to change the engine gasket (whatever that means).

Oh, and I mustn't forget to pick up my dress from the laundry for my weekend girls' night out, and oh yes, return Mom's call too. How can there still be traffic at this hour? It's been such a crappy day. I wonder when it will dawn on my boss that I'm the next Sheryl Sandberg.

Or maybe Oprah Winfrey—I've got her hair too. When will these long work hours stop?

8.30 p.m.

I'm still stuck in traffic and I'm so hungry, but I can't think of a recipe that involves zero thinking and only five hand movements (including stirring).

I'm tired of takeout.

If only I had someone waiting for me at home, giving me a huge hug and holding out a plate of hot pasta as I enter the house. Hmm . . . pasta.

Yes, pasta. Steaming hot, cooked to al dente creamy perfection.

9.20 p.m.

I drain the penne pasta into a deep-bottomed white plate and grab my pepper mill; two rounds of freshly ground pepper and a pinch of sea salt does it for seasoning.

As I stir in a dollop of pesto, I feel the stress of the day begin to evaporate.

A generous sprinkle of grated Parmesan cheese and a delicate garnish of some olive-green pumpkin seeds—bellissimo!

9.30 p.m.

Yup, that's dinner in well under thirty minutes.

As I cuddle up on my favourite spot on the sofa, kick off my pink bunny-head softies, and dig my fork into a freshly made hot plate of pesto pasta, I feel reassured and relaxed.

No matter how chaotic my day has been, I've still got the verve and skills to whip up a quick and simple meal that leaves me feeling `a-ma-zing!`

Every day as I drive home, a similar frantic internal monologue repeats in my head. Whether I'm happy, on the move, or feeling adventurous, there's always a recipe running through my mind. There's a sense of satisfaction in knowing that no matter how my day went, I could always whip up a quick-fix hot, fresh meal.

How did this come to be? Let's start with where it all began...

Most of my earliest childhood memories revolve around food experiences. Running eagerly from the school bus, flinging my school bag onto the floor, and heading straight into the kitchen to check what's for lunch; waking up to the aromas of tempered spices as breakfast is being prepared; 'helping out' in the kitchen and trying to poke my chubby little fingers into the dough my mom had left aside to rest; licking freshly whipped cake batter off the whisk . . . I'm also certain the fact that we cooked three different types of Indian regional cuisines played a role in broadening my palate and appreciation of differing textures and cooking methods.

My mom and dad hail from two very different parts of India: Mom is from Mumbai, a popular cosmopolitan metro, and my dad from tropical Kerala, rich in Ayurvedic rituals and also the land of the coconuts. Also raising me was my nanny who was from the coastal state of Mangalore. From cooking curries in traditional mud pots, to paper-thin crêpes made from coconut milk served with chicken prepared with freshly roasted and ground spices, to fragrant turmeric and coriander rice pulaos—we had it all under one roof.

However, as the years went by, my love of food remained confined to home-cooked meals and kitchen moseying. Post high school, though I was considering medicine, my folks and I attended an education fair to 'see what's out there'. And what was out there was the hospitality management school that wrote the story of the next four years of my life. I still remember my first day in the kitchen during Food & Beverage 101, learning the difference between macédoine and julienne while cutting carrots, and worrying if I should have dropped the idea of becoming a doctor. However, to my amazement, I turned out to be a natural in the kitchen. I dug my head into Philip Pauli's *Classical Cooking the Modern Way: Methods and Techniques* like it was New York's best-selling thriller novel. Night and day, I learned about the French thirteen-course meals, the nine basic cooking methods, types of knives, and other such topics. Suddenly, it was all coming together: What I had learnt at home had an art, logic, and science to it, and hotel school further consolidated and expanded my knowledge.

Next up was a short stint as a transfer student in Lausanne, Switzerland. This was my first experience of international travel as a young adult, and life really began opening up. As I stumbled upon age-old family-run chocolatiers and cheesemakers, and learned how sharing a meal with friends could narrow cultural differences, I discovered a whole new dimension to cooking and eating.

After graduation and stepping into my first

full-time job, I was soon heavily laden with international travel and responsibilities. My ultimate de-stressor? Baking. Nothing was more calming and soothing than to come home from work and bake a cake. Soon I found myself toggling between internet browser windows at work, researching the best pastry schools in the world. I had a sense I wanted to become a baker and open my own café serving hand-crafted coffees, artisanal breads, and freshly made home bakes—until one fine day I had to decide between graduate business school in Spain or The French Pastry School in the United States. Pastry school took a backseat, and I flew to Madrid where I spent the best two years of my life.

While graduate school was intense, I still found my way to new culinary experiences. I learnt how to sniff and swoosh wine in my mouth like the connoisseurs at a vineyard in Valdepeñas, savour the taste of Manchego cheese drizzled with cold-pressed extra virgin olive oil, relish the *pan con tomate* crusty breads smothered with muddled garlic-tomato spread, get tipsy on Pisco Sours introduced to me by my Chilean peers, and enjoy life guilt-free as the Spanish do while they make merry around vino, tapas, and salsa. During school breaks, I ate my way through Europe, from savouring the delicate macarons from Ladurée in Paris, to guzzling limoncello shots on the Amalfi coast in Italy.

After my MBA, as I began to settle down on my

home turf—Dubai—and as I took globetrotting more seriously, a prominent part of my exploration of any country centred around culinary experiences, including sampling new foods, visiting farmers' markets, signing up for food walks, and reading up on the country's food history. I loved discovering new truths about cultures by means of their eating habits, cooking methods, fresh produce, and tastes. Eventually, and as an organic progression, I set up my blog 'The Munching Traveler', where I narrated my encounters and experiences.

As a food and travel blogger, I began to appear as a media rep interviewing cookbook authors at the Emirates Literature Festival. Conversations with personalities like Ken Hom, Antonio Carluccio, Madhur Jaffrey, Willie Harcourt-Cooze, and Rachel Allen were inspirational and gave me a glimpse into their world as chefs and cookbook authors. I wanted a piece of the passion they exuded as they spoke about their lives and their love of cooking.

As years passed and the corporate world pressed on, I leaned further into the place where I felt most comfortable, most grounded—my kitchen. As all the bits and pieces of my experiences began to amalgamate, it led me to write this cookbook. It's for you, a woman who has her A-game in the boardroom, is a fantastic confidante to her friends, but is perhaps a bit soft-kneed in the kitchen! Whether it's whipping up a meal in your high heels or PJs, this book guides you to a place where you can twirl, create, sing, and chill out. From recipes I grew up on as a child, to collecting food-stained recipe notes, curating some of my top faves from my girlfriends, and inventing my own shortcuts and hacks, I'm here to show you how to get skilled and sassy in the kitchen. I'm never out of a reason to find myself in my happiest place—the kitchen—and I want to help you find your happy self there, too. You're on your way to living your best life yet!

This book is my ode to you, girlfriend.
—Delne
·xoxo·

THE HOW-TO GUIDE TO GETTING SASSY AND SKILLED

—

YOUR KITCHEN DOES MORE FOR YOU THAN A MASSAGE EVER COULD!

—

YOUR KITCHEN, YOUR SANCTUARY

It's not very often that we think of our kitchen as a sanctuary.

For most of us, sanctuaries are overpriced spas we go to when in need of some serious TLC. But the kitchen? We tiptoe in out of sheer necessity: when we want to fix a quick bite, grab a drink, or throw out the trash.

When you think about it, your kitchen does more for you than a cocoa-butter hot-stone massage ever could. It's where you get your source of energy: food. Maintaining an inviting and calming kitchen is key, especially when we want to get in, prep, toss, stir, and get out with a plated meal in our hands in no time at all.

Kitchens are one of the first things I notice about someone's home (sorry, I know that's a tad creepy). Once I've got a glimpse of the kitchen, I start imagining spices flying all over the place, uncompartmentalized fridges, jumbled plates and glasses . . . and here's my pet peeve: the 'stuff' behind the kitchen doors! Yikes.

Your starting point to get whipping in the kitchen is to create a space you're happy walking into and that doesn't get you all wired up. Making cooking fun and stress-free goes way beyond the few minutes or hours you spend in your kitchen. It includes everything you do **before** and **after** the actual cooking. You may have made yourself a great meal in record time, but the dishes in the sink still need to be done, the next day's ingredients are missing, and frankly, you're bored of the few standard flavours you've been rotating. Not that fun then, eh?

I realized this soon enough and began to micro-analyse what it is that keeps me sassy and skilled in the kitchen. And no, I'm not suggesting you turn yourself into a flawless Stepford Wife. You don't have to be perfect, but the kitchen experience has to be something you enjoy, which you will if you kick butt at it. Whether it's planning, playing hostess, or stirring up a meal, this book contains pointers and tips that help me keep my mojo on. I can assure you, waking-up in the morning and entering a freshly scented, organised, and spotless kitchen gives you a good feeling. It reminds you that you're in control of your life, you can take care of yourself, and that you're altogether fabulous.

Believe me when I say there's no genetically inherited talent involved in maintaining your kitchen as an inviting and stress-free space. It just takes a little bit of practice and care till it eventually becomes a habit.

1. WASH AS YOU GO

Clean the dishes after every meal or, better still, as you work.

I will never forget F&B 101 during my hospitality management days when I thought I was Jamie Oliver in the female form. I was searing the steaks with rosemary and garlic-infused butter, the aromas wafting through our student-run kitchen. I could even sense the occasional appreciative nods. I used to boast I never needed a thermometer to gauge the temperature of meat and could tell its cooking degree with just one finger touch. Hah! Beat that, I would tell myself.

Until one day our chef instructor called out a loud 'STOP right there, Del' in his thick English accent. He was so firm in his command that I froze, turned off the gas, and looked at him nervously. At this point, the kitchen buzz silenced, and every student was looking at me. Do you recognize that feeling of knowing something's gone wrong but you're oblivious of what it could be? 'Turn around and look at your sink,' he said. 'Till you get that cleaned to the very bottom, you aren't turning that flame on again.'

I was so embarrassed to have been called out on something so simple. In hindsight, it was a great lesson that totally changed my working system while cooking. To date, every time something is baking or simmering on low heat, I use the time to clean up the dishes in the sink. A basic rule of thumb is to avoid stacking dishes until the next meal, because then you would have two meals' worth of dishes to take care of! No overnight slumber, which means don't leave your dishes in the sink through the night.

Make it a habit to wash all that's in the sink, so you can wake up to a fresh start in the morning.

2. KEEP YOUR CUTTING BOARDS APART

If you looked at your chopping boards under a microscope, you would shudder at the tiny bits of food stuck between the grooves, decaying in shades of green and grey.

Maintaining different cutting boards, each dedicated to one food type (raw meats, vegetables, dairy, fish, cooked food), prevents food groups mixing, plus you know which board to scrub the most and which one is probably okay with just a wipe down. IKEA has some handy and colourful boards. If you can't manage many, at least maintain two or three different boards. Here's a basic guide for you to consider, plus they throw a splash of colour into your kitchen!

- **Green:** Fruits and vegetables
- **Red:** Raw poultry and meat
- **Blue:** Raw fish
- **Yellow:** Cooked meats
- **White:** Bakery and dairy

3. SWEEP AWAY

After you've prepared a meal, sweep the kitchen floor as the final wrap-up act.

You may feel like Cinderella, but hey, she used to sing her way through. So, no shame there, girl, because keeping your kitchen looking clean is the best thing you can do to honour that space.

4. CHECK, CHECK

Make it a regular habit to check through your dry store and fridge for any expired foods.

Doing this will help you see which items are nearing their expiry date so you can plan to use those ingredients in your upcoming meals and thereby lessen food waste.

5. GREASE-FREE ZONES

Except for the bowls, glasses, and other dishes you use regularly, move all dishes to a closed cabinet away from the stove.

You may have noticed a slightly greasy feel when you pick up a dish you don't use that often. It feels sticky because of its proximity to the stove and all the grease particles that get dispersed during cooking. So, keep what you use often in the kitchen within reach, and store the rest elsewhere. Doing this reduces clutter too!

6. SMART ACCESS

Sort and organise your pots and pans, including the lids.

It drives me nuts when I have to run around the kitchen, opening every cabinet and getting down on my knees to look for a particular pot (I call this doing kitchen squats).

Lining up your pots and lids and storing them in order of depth or width will help you pick the ones you want to use and save you the rummaging.

7. TICK-TOCK

 A clock helps you manage your time well in the kitchen.

Also, hang a calendar to note down important dates, and keep a notepad and pen handy to jot down items to buy as and when you notice you're out of stock, or even to capture those great ideas and thoughts brewing in your mind as you're stirring something.

Who said showers were the only thinking spots?

8. FRIDGE MANAGEMENT

A picture-perfect fridge, the kind that's right out of Nigella Lawson's cookbook, can be your reality too.

I call it fridge management, and it simply means assigning a purpose for each shelf. For example, the top shelf for me is for everyday items such as butter, cheese, milk, etc.

Invest in glass or plastic storage containers in different sizes. Use them to store any leftovers, ensuring you use the right size of container to maximise space in the fridge.

Don't leave any food uncovered. This will avoid unpleasant odours and prevent food from turning dry.

At the end of the day, spend a few minutes arranging the containers in your fridge to optimize space.

Always, always, and always survey your leftovers before whipping up anything new.

9. THROW IN SOME COLOUR

The best way to add a bit of colour to your kitchen is to have a small plant in the corner or a small bunch of fresh flowers.

Plants and flowers represent life and they provide a fresh feel to your kitchen. If my brother can grow herbs like basil and coriander (#truestory) so can you; plus, herbs come in super handy when cooking.

10. THROW IN A LITTLE FUN

Fridge magnets, fun aprons, kitchen curios!

Some may say it's clutter, but that depends on how you arrange them on your fridge and on your shelves. On my fridge, I have a few magnets with cheeky quotes and from countries I've travelled to. They're often great conversation starters.

My favourite one is deceptively simple:
Life begins after coffee. That one is from Sant' Eustachio cafe in Rome, founded in 1938.
They claim to serve the best coffee in the world, and if someone points out to that fridge magnet, I'll happily brag about my experience sipping an espresso just next to the Pantheon.

11. PLAN YOUR SUPERMARKET VISITS

There was a time when I used my shopping cart around the supermarket aisles like a Pacman game.

With no order to my shopping list, grocery visits were a real mission. The worst bit about a disorganised shopping list is that you end up with everything in your cart except what was on your list . . . Yup, guilty as charged.

Write up your shopping lists exactly how a supermarket is laid out—by food categories. That means listing your items to purchase under the suggested broad categories, as follows:

→ Bakery
→ Dairy
→ Fresh meats
→ Dry pantry (tins, cans, packets), and nuts
→ Fruits, vegetables, and herbs
→ Frozen food

You get the idea. Doing this means that once you're at a particular aisle and you look at your shopping list, you see exactly what you need to grab and you won't have to double back five minutes later for a forgotten item.

12. WHERE'S YOUR FAVOURITE PLAYLIST?

It can get pretty boring cooking with only the sounds of your neighbour's kids running around the floor above your kitchen ceiling, the traffic buzz, or even your friend on speaker going on and on about how she can't decide between lilac and violet for her date night.

My top recommendation?

Invest in a great Bluetooth speaker and turn on your favourite playlist. Sing along and do a little dance as the tunes lift your mood, get you smiling, and help you focus on the lovely meal you're working up an appetite for.

13. DON'T BE AFRAID TO EXPERIMENT

Never, ever be afraid to experiment.

Heard the expression "What doesn't kill you makes you stronger"? The same logic applies here, girl. Extend your comfort zone, expand your horizons, and go for it. Try a new flavour, a new cooking method, a new ingredient. What's the worst that can happen? Ken Hom, the famous Chinese-American chef, once said to me, "Always taste the food and if you don't like it, you can still spit it out. But at least try, feel, and observe the flavours before making a decision that you don't like something". Words of wisdom I always pay heed to when experimenting in the kitchen.

14. SEMI-COOK, PREP, AND MAKE ROOM FOR LEFTOVERS

Most recipes can be made in parts; for instance, marinate the meats, boil the chicken, and chop the vegetables.

These preps can be done ahead of time and brought out to come to room temperature just before you're ready to prepare the dish. Also, always assess if you can make a little extra for another meal or as a side dish. Remember, the best thing about leftovers is that you can convert them into a whole new dish.

15. MISE-EN-PLACE IS GOLD

Mise-en-place is a French term that refers to getting your ingredients and dishes ready well before you begin cooking.

This is F&B 101 and it is a golden tip. My mom never quite got why I would get all the ingredients portioned and ready, and all the necessary dishes lined up. It drove her nuts, but preparing your mise-en-place allows you to quickly move from one ingredient to the next without spending time weighing or chopping during the cooking process.

You may find preparing your mise-en-place time consuming at first, but soon it will become second nature, and you won't be willing to cook without getting it done beforehand.

16. SMART MEASUREMENTS

Have you ever watched cooking shows where the chefs use their hands so gracefully for measurements?

They either sprinkle, add a few, splash, dust, grab a handful, or even combine spices as they go. This is known as estimation, and it comes from a little trial and error, some tasting, and some gut feeling.

The first step is to always taste every ingredient to get familiar with it, and eventually you will develop the ability to sense if a little more of that ingredient will enhance or mar the other flavours. Second, start visualizing flavours, because you can almost feel them on your tongue.

This may seem funny at start, but if you focus and embrace the process, very soon you won't need a set of measuring spoons. If you want to get sassy in the kitchen, you've got to use your hands and trust all your five senses.

Here's a quick guide to get you started with estimating:

- **A pinch:**
  picked up with the thumb, index, and middle finger
- **A dash:**
  one splash
- **A knob:**
  1 tablespoon
- **One serving of fat:**
  a single thumb
- **One serving of protein:**
  roughly the size of your palm
- **One serving of rice:**
  a cupped hand
- **One serving of veggies:**
  two clenched fists
- **One inch:**
  one-third the length of your index finger
- **Salts:**
  taste first to see how salty your salt is
  (they vary, trust me!)
- **Seasoning:**
  first add a little, then a little more
- **½ lime, squeezed:**
  roughly 1 teaspoon of juice

17. BEFORE BEDTIME SANITY CHECK

☐ Cleaned the kitchen counter?
☐ Swept the floor?
☐ No dishes in the sink?
☐ Organised the fridge?
☐ Thrown out the trash?
☐ Turned off the gas/electric supply
   to the stove?

Yes to all?
Go ahead and turn the lights off.

Good night!

BREAKFAST QUICKIES

1.	GRILLED CHEESE & PBJ SANDWICH	42
2.	JONU'S PERFECT SCRAMBLED EGGS	44
3.	BACON AND VEGGIE OMELETTE ON-THE-GO	46
4.	ALL-IN-ONE BREAKFAST PANCAKES	47
5.	APPLE CINNAMON OATS IN FIVE	48
6.	DESI VEG VERMICELLI	50
7.	GREEN MUNG BEAN CRÊPES	52
8.	SAVOURY FLATTENED RICE (POHA)	54
9.	PINA COLADA QUINOA FRUIT SALAD	56
10.	HIMALAYAN PORRIDGE BOWL	57

BREAKFAST QUICKIES

Thoughtful but quick breakfasts eaten at the counter or ready to go.

Good morning Delna, time to wake up, it's a new day, make it count . . . Good morning Delna, time to wake up, it's a new day, make it count . . .

I seemed to think recording my voice as the alarm tone, like a note-to-self message, would magically get me out of bed at 5 a.m. But every morning as the alarm goes off, I curse myself for such an annoying idea. Bam, I hit snooze. And then again two minutes later, and then again and again for the next hour.

Oh shoot! I'm late again.

As I brush my teeth and lather up my curls at the same time, the usual "what's for breakfast?" thought runs through my mind. If you're anything like me, breakfast is paramount. It's one event I really look forward to, and it's what gets me kicking some bottoms throughout the day. But with just forty minutes left before I'm due at the office, I'm often seen running out of the house with one heel in my hand, zipping through traffic, and finally arriving at the office sheepishly holding a take-away croissant from the local coffee shop.

I got tired of eating cold croissants day in and day out, so I started to carve out a few minutes in the morning to whip up some freshly made breakfasts at home. Today, I always, always come back to these breakfast ideas because apart from being absolutely yummy, they're ready in no time, and I feel I've earned brownie points for making breakfast while applying lipstick. These dishes are also planned and prepared to be packed into my little meal carry box and nibbled on during a meeting, at my desk, or even as a snack later.

So, ditch the donut-on-the-go and bring on some **DARN. GOOD. BREAKFAST!**

—

MAKEUP AFTER BREAKFAST. ALWAYS. HAPPY TUMMIES TURN YOU BEAUTIFUL INSIDE OUT.

—

GRILLED CHEESE & PBJ SANDWICH

SERVING

Serves: **1**

INGREDIENTS

2 slices
German rye,
farmer's bread,
or sourdough

2 tablespoons
crunchy peanut
butter

2 tablespoons
your favourite
fruit jam

3 or 4 slices
your favourite
cheese

Butter, at room
temperature

Honey,
for drizzling
(optional)

Sandwiches are super simple, no-brainer breakfasts. One of my favourite grilled sandwiches is none other than the hot-diggity PB&J (peanut butter and jelly) sandwich.

I instinctively felt the combination of grilled cheese with peanut butter and jelly would be a killah twist on the traditional version. I've even managed to make this sandwich on sleepy mornings when I can barely keep my eyes open, let alone draw a half-decent eyeliner stroke.

I've tried this recipe with cheddar, mozzarella, provolone, and Swiss, and all turned out amazingly cheesy with that nutty crunch and fruity jam sweetness. These are no ordinary PB&Js because who likes simple and boring anyways? Oh, please don't cringe, but I occasionally swap the fruit jam with Nutella. It's for the chocolate bravehearts.

METHOD

1. Spread one bread slice with the peanut butter. Spread the other slice with the fruit jam.

2. Lay the cheese on both slices of bread, making sure to cover the bread well. Don't worry if the cheese falls over the edges of the bread.

3. Put the bread slices together, sandwiching the spreads and cheese, and brush a little butter on the top and bottom of the sandwich.

4. Place the sandwich in a sandwich grill and toast until both sides are golden, crisp and the cheese has melted.

5. Serve warm, straight from the grill. Drizzle with a little honey (if using).

Don't have a sandwich maker/grill? Fret not. You can work the same magic on a skillet (you'll just miss the grill marks). **Toast the sandwich on a preheated skillet** until you get a golden crisp on both sides.

Better still, **hold the sandwich down with a weight** such as a heavy glass plate or a mug filled with water. This way the sandwich compresses, which helps melt the cheese.

JONU'S PERFECT SCRAMBLED EGGS

SERVING

Serves: **1**

INGREDIENTS

2 eggs

Freshly ground
black pepper

Sea salt

Knob butter,
plus **½ teaspoon**

1 teaspoon
fresh cream

I still have clear memories of days spent at my Aunt Veronica's home where my cousin Jonathan (Jonu, as we call him) always had these really fluffy, pale yellow eggs. Each time I stayed at my aunt's, I hustled to get served "Jonu's eggs".

Years later, I realized it was nothing but good 'ol scrambled eggs! It doesn't matter if I was six years old then or thirty-something today, when I'm with my family we still have conversations that go something like this: "What's for breakfast? Jonu's eggs or omelettes?"

Each bite reminds me of my younger days and that sense of love, security, and heart-warming togetherness.

As eggs cook quickly, always maintain low heat to carefully manage the texture while preparing.

METHOD

1. Crack the eggs into a bowl and whisk them with a fork until frothy.

2. Season the eggs with a little pepper and salt and whisk again.

3. Place a small pan on low heat and add the knob of butter.

4. When the butter has melted, pour the eggs into the pan.

5. As you see the sides of the eggs begin to crisp very slightly, use a spatula in quick swirling movements to 'loosen' the liquid part of the eggs; you will see small egg curds begin to form.

6. Use the spatula in slow, gentle, up-down strokes to stir the eggs, still on low heat. Just before the eggs begin to get solid, add the cream and the remaining ½ teaspoon of butter and continue to cook, using the same strokes.

7. Turn the heat off when the eggs are still creamy as they will continue cooking in the residual heat.

8. Butter a piece of toasted bread, top it with the eggs, and sprinkle with sea salt and pepper, if preferred.

SASS!

As you patiently stir the eggs, instead of staring down blankly at the pan, **use the time to think about the day that lies ahead** or three reasons why today is a great day to be alive.

Use every moment, girl!

BACON AND VEGGIE OMELETTE ON-THE-GO

SERVING

Serves: **1**

INGREDIENTS

3 eggs

Salt

Freshly ground black pepper

Knob butter

3 tablespoons bell pepper, finely chopped

½ medium onion, finely chopped

½ medium tomato, finely chopped

2 or 3 button mushrooms, finely chopped

2 beef or turkey bacon strips, roughly chopped

Some dishes are invented by chance or necessity. The other day I was racing against the clock and my colleague was frantically calling me for last-minute checks on our morning presentation, but all that was on my mind was a full English breakfast.

If only. So, on days like that, instead of cooking my eggs, veggies, and bacon separately, I throw them all into the pan together, put a lid on it, turn the heat down low, and head back into my room to finish my makeup.

The result is a wholesome, tasty meal that is almost like a frittata quickie. Creativity under pressure works like magic!

METHOD

1. Crack the eggs into a bowl, season with salt and pepper, and whisk until the eggs are frothy and pale yellow.

2. Place a pan on low heat and melt the butter in it. Add the bell peppers, onion, tomato, mushrooms, and bacon; season with a little salt and pepper. Stir fry for a couple of minutes until the vegetables begin to soften.

3. Pour the whisked eggs into the pan and swirl the pan to evenly cover the vegetables and bacon. Leave the heat on low, and cover the pan with a lid.

4. In about 5 minutes, remove the lid and you'll see the eggs are set. Slide the omelette out of the pan, ready to be packed or served warm.

If you like your eggs with a little bit of cheese, grate some cheese over the eggs just before you cover the pan.

SKILL

On a high-protein diet? Try this recipe using three egg whites, **no yolks.**

To separate the whites from the yolks, crack an egg over a bowl and immediately scoot the yolk into one half of the shell, allowing the egg white to fall into the bowl. Now shift the egg yolk to the other half shell while the egg white continues to drip into the bowl. Easy, isn't it?

ALL-IN-ONE BREAKFAST PANCAKES

A well-made pancake can make me smile wide, even on grumpy mornings. Oh my, the joy of seeing those little bubbles forming in the pancake batter, and the wafts of vanilla scenting my kitchen.

My recipe has all the typical brekkie ingredients packed into every bite— nuts, coconut, fruit, and oats all whipped up. Short on time? Make the batter the previous night and whip it in the morning, using milk or water to adjust the consistency if you need to, just before adding to the skillet.

Remember, you can save the batter for up to a day if you don't have time to cook the entire batch immediately.

SERVING

Makes: **8 to 9 pancakes**

INGREDIENTS

1 cup milk

1 cup all-purpose flour

2 tablespoons freshly coconut, grated

1 tablespoon regular oats

½ ripe banana, mashed

1 egg

4 to 6 cashew nuts (or any nut), soaked in water

1 teaspoon vanilla essence

1 to 2 teaspoons sugar

Pinch baking powder

Pinch salt

Butter

METHOD

1. Pour the milk into a blender, followed by all of the remaining ingredients (except the butter). Blend until you get a smooth, easy to pour consistency.

2. Place a skillet on low heat, and smear a small knob of butter in the skillet to melt. When melted, pour ½ or 1 ladleful of batter into the skillet. With the back of the ladle, move the batter in a circular motion to create a round shape. Cover the skillet with a lid.

3. After a minute, lift the lid to see if small bubbles are forming in the batter while it begins to brown on the bottom. When you see the sides firming up, loosen the pancake sides with a spatula and flip the pancake to brown the other side. Repeat until all the batter has been used. Serve as is or with a drizzle of honey or maple syrup.

SKILL

Trouble swirling the batter to make perfect circles? No sweat. **Create irregular circles**— there's no pressure to be perfect! If you're really dedicated to geometry, in your free time you can practice making swirls using Greek yoghurt on an unheated skillet.

APPLE CINNAMON OATS IN FIVE

SERVING

Serves: **1**

INGREDIENTS

½ red or green apple, finely chopped

½ teaspoon butter

Honey

Pinch ground cinnamon

Pinch ground nutmeg (optional)

1 cup full cream milk or almond milk

4 tablespoons steel cut or regular oats

1 tablespoon almonds, pecans, or walnuts, roughly chopped

Pinch salt

I like oats, but the thought of standing over the stove and stirring until it's cooked makes me roll my eyes.

Hello, microwave!

If serving immediately, pour into a mug (I love eating from a mug!). If you're going to be eating it later, you can microwave the oats in a glass storage container directly and let it cool down as you get your bag ready for the day ahead.

Snap the lid on the container and it's ready to be enjoyed first thing at your desk, before you deep dive into your inbox.

METHOD

1. In a glass bowl, combine the apple, butter, honey to taste, cinnamon, and nutmeg (if using). Use a spoon to stir the ingredients until the apples are well coated with the mixture.

2. Place the bowl in the microwave and cook for 1 minute. Remove and check; the apples should be slightly softened. If not, return to the microwave and cook for a few more seconds.

3. Add half the milk, the oats, nuts, and salt to the bowl and stir. Once again place the bowl in the microwave, cover with a microwave safe lid and cook in the microwave for 3 minutes.

4. Remove the bowl from the microwave, drizzle with more honey if you like, and stir in the remaining milk. Let the oats cool down for a couple of minutes before eating.

I'm all about a generous drizzle for my oats.

SASS!

Have fun with combinations: Dust with cocoa and freshly grated coconut, add raisins instead of honey, or even muddle some berries on top with a dollop of fresh cream.

Trust your taste buds and go crazy!

DESI VEG VERMICELLI

INGREDIENTS

1 to 1½ tablespoons olive oil

1 teaspoon mustard seeds

½ teaspoon split white gram *(urad dal)* (optional)

8 curry leaves

1 green chilli, finely chopped

¼ cup carrots, finely chopped

¼ cup green beans, finely chopped

¼ cup canned corn kernels

Pinch ground turmeric

Salt

1 cup vermicelli

2 cups water, boiled and kept warm

1 teaspoon lime juice, freshly squeezed

1 tablespoon fresh coriander, finely chopped

Desi means 'ours' or 'local' in Hindi, and we Indians love our spices; we make sure spice finds its way into every dish. Desi Vermicelli is every Indian household's go-to breakfast because it's light, packs well for later as a snack, and is ready in a jiffy.

My humbled-down version is simple, quick, and made in fewer than fifteen minutes. It can be pushed a notch higher with extra veggies and peanuts.

In case of leftovers, pack some for a snack or light dinner option. No wastage, love!

Or you can use ¾ cup frozen mixed vegetables.

Wondering if adding meat to this would do it justice? Heck yeah! Throw in some chopped frozen sausage or some minced chicken.

Just make sure to add the meat before adding the vegetables to give the meat ample time to cook.

SERVING

Serves: **2**

METHOD

1. Place a saucepan on medium heat and pour in the oil.

2. As the oil heats, add the mustard seeds and wait until they crackle. Follow with the split white gram (if using), and stir until it begins to turn slightly golden brown. Lower the heat, add the curry leaves and green chilli, and stir fry for a few seconds.

3. Add the carrots, beans, and corn, followed by the turmeric and salt to taste. Continue to stir fry for a few minutes on low heat.

4. Add the vermicelli and gently mix with the vegetables. Add the water and bring it to a boil on medium heat.

5. As the water comes to the boil, reduce the heat slightly and wait until the water just starts to dry. Turn the heat off and stir once. Cover the pan with a lid and let the vermicelli rest for 10 to 15 minutes.

6. When done, the vermicelli should be slightly moist but still pull apart easily.

7. Stir in the lime juice, garnish with the coriander and let rest for a few minutes before serving.

GREEN MUNG BEAN CRÊPES

SERVING

Makes:
8 or 9 crêpes

INGREDIENTS

½ cup full green mung beans *(moong dal)*

½-inch piece fresh ginger

½ medium onion, roughly chopped

2 green chillies, roughly chopped

1 tablespoon yellow Bengal gram powder *(chana dal)*

Salt

Olive oil, for frying

This vegetarian breakfast recipe is a pocket-friendly protein option. It's also easy, great tasting, and allergen-free. Mung *(moong dal)* beans are one of the most commonly used lentils in India, and we've learnt to create our very own version of crêpes using them.

Initially, this was a recipe I kept for weekends because I always thought it took time. Then one day I saw my mom make it and I was like *what?! No way. This is easy-peasy.* As smart prep, once you have the soaked mung beans ready, go ahead and prepare the batter the previous night.

Don't let go of a killer combination with coconut chutney because of time! While you wait for the crêpes to cook, use the time to make some fresh, tasty, and healthy coconut chutney. Check out the recipe on page 149.

On a weekend, visit your local mill or the loose herb and spice section in supermarkets. **Get familiar with the different types of pulses and lentils.**

Pick them, feel them, and even taste a few as is. The more familiar you get with the look, feel and the names, the less scary a recipe becomes.

METHOD

1. Wash the mung beans well before soaking in about 1 cup of water for 4 hours or, better still, overnight.

2. Once soaked, put the mung beans into a blender along with the water in which the beans were soaked. Add the ginger, onion, green chillies, and enough additional water (about 1 cup); blend well to achieve a smooth pouring consistency.

3. Pour the batter into a bowl and thoroughly stir in the Bengal gram powder. Finally, add salt to taste.

4. Place a skillet or frying pan on low heat. When the pan has slightly warmed up, add about ½ teaspoon of olive oil and use a tissue to smear the surface of the skillet with the oil. Now, pour a ladleful of batter into the skillet and use the back of the ladle in circular motions to spread the batter evenly.

5. Still on low heat, lightly trace the edges of the crêpes with a little oil. You will notice the oil begin to slightly sizzle. Cover the crêpe with a lid for a couple of minutes.

6. Remove the lid, and when you notice the sides turning crisp, use a spatula to loosen the edges and flip the crêpe. Wait for 1 to 2 minutes and remove from the heat. Repeat until you have used all the batter. Best served with coconut chutney, or Greek yoghurt too.

You can store the excess batter for another day if you're short on time.

SAVOURY FLATTENED RICE (POHA)

INGREDIENTS

Salt

1 small bowl water, at room temperature

1 cup flattened rice flakes, rinsed and drained

1 tablespoon olive oil

¼ teaspoon mustard seeds

1 medium onion, finely chopped

5 or 6 curry leaves

2 green chillies, slit in half

¼ teaspoon ground turmeric

Handful roasted peanuts, skin on

2 big pinches coriander leaves and stems, finely chopped for garnish

1 small lime, juice squeezed

Freshly grated coconut

Poha, or flattened rice, is one ingredient I highly recommend you keep in your dry pantry. These are rice grains (white or brown) that have been flattened or 'beaten' to a light, dry flake.

With a little bit of water, the flakes swell and can be used either in savoury dishes or as a sweet with some milk and sugar. The North Indian version of this dish is a full-hearted breakfast with coconut, vegetables, peanuts, and herbs.

My really simple version has all the key ingredients and nutrients the fitness gurus harp on about: peanut protein, good fats from freshly grated coconut, turmeric as an antioxidant and anti-inflammatory, rice as a good complex carb, and even coriander with its minerals and fibre. What more could you need to start your day on a high and healthy note?

↳ In a small pan, dry roast the peanuts for 5 to 7 minutes. Keep stirring. Or buy pre-roasted peanuts.

SERVING

Serves: **2**

METHOD

1. Put a pinch of salt in the bowl of water. Soak the rice flakes in the water for 1 to 2 seconds. Drain the rice flakes and set them aside.

2. In a deep-bottomed pan, heat the oil on medium heat. Wave your hand gently above the pan, and when you feel heat from the oil (well below smoking point), add the mustard seeds.

3. Once the mustard seeds have crackled, add the onion, curry leaves, and chillies and fry until the onion is translucent. Stir in the turmeric then add the roasted peanuts. Continue to stir on medium heat.

4. Add the rice flakes, stir well and check the seasoning (add salt if required). Reduce the heat and cover the pan with a lid for 1 to 2 minutes.

5. Turn the heat off, and add the chopped coriander, lime juice, and grated coconut.

I love eating Poha accompanied by a cup of chai

SKILL

When using coriander or any herb for garnish, **don't discard the stems!** They are packed with flavour.

Also, instead of struggling with holding the herbs together as you chop on a cutting board, simply hold the rinsed herbs over the dish and snip away using **scissors**.

PINA COLADA QUINOA FRUIT SALAD

SERVING

Serves: **2 to 3**

INGREDIENTS

½ cup water, at room temperature

¼ cup quinoa

Pinch salt

3 cups your favourite fruits, chopped in equal size—make sure you use varied colours and berries too

½ cup mixed nuts, roughly chopped

For the dressing

2 tablespoons coconut cream

4 tablespoons pineapple juice

2 tablespoons honey

Fresh mint leaves, finely chopped

I'm one of those people who eat fruit only because I have to. I remember staring down at my fruit bowl one day thinking, how boring can this be?

I mean, don't get me wrong. I know fruit is great for the body, but I eat them because I need them and not because I want them. One day, on a girl's night out while sipping some Pina Colada, the thought struck me—how about a pineapple-coconut punch to my boring fruit bowl?

With a few takes in the kitchen, here's my rendition on making just another fruit salad bowl more 'exciting'.

METHOD

1. Bring the water to a boil; add the quinoa and salt. Boil for about 5 minutes and then simmer for about 10 minutes or until the quinoa is cooked. Fluff the quinoa with a fork, then set aside to cool.

2. Make the dressing by first whisking the coconut cream in a bowl until it is smooth and creamy. Add the pineapple juice, honey, and mint to the coconut cream and whisk it all together.

3. Place the fruit in a bowl, and add in the nuts and quinoa (which should now be at room temperature). Stir in the dressing and mix well. Serve at room temperature or keep chilled in the refrigerator.

SKILL

When cooking grains, remember the 1:2 ratio. **For every 1 cup of grain, double the quantity of water when boiling** (i.e., for ¼ cup of quinoa, use ½ cup of water).

This way you never, ever go wrong ending up with undercooked or mushy grains.

HIMALAYAN PORRIDGE BOWL

SERVING

Serves: **1**

INGREDIENTS

Knob butter

4 tablespoons cracked or broken wheat *(dalia)*

1 to 2 teaspoons sugar

Pinch salt

1¼ cups milk

Pinch ground cinnamon

I was twenty-three when I took my first trip to the Himalayan region of India. I wanted to experience something different, and the idea of trekking the mountains was intriguing.

From that day to this, I make it a point to visit the mountains every year to soak in snow-capped views, breathe in crisp air, meet some lovely village folks and even ex-urbanites. But most of all, I go to eat hyper local, fresh, organic food.

There's something about the freshness of the ingredients and the love that people put into their cooking that makes every single spoonful mouth-watering, even if it's a simple bowl of porridge. I still remember the first time I had porridge at one of the homestays in Sonapani— that buttery, crunchy, creamy, aromatic bowl is entrenched in my senses.

To this day, whenever I make this porridge I get nostalgic and long to be in the Himalayas.

METHOD

1. Put a saucepan on low heat and melt the butter. Add the broken wheat and roast it in the melted butter until it turns slightly brown and begins to release a nutty aroma. This could take 3 to 4 minutes.

2. Add the sugar and salt and stir for a few seconds, then pour in the milk.

3. Increase the heat to medium and bring everything to a boil, then lower the heat and let the milk simmer for 10 to 12 minutes. Stir occasionally to check if the wheat is cooked; it becomes slightly soft but still retains a crunchy texture.

4. Turn off the heat and set aside to cool slightly. Eat warm and don't forget to dust with some cinnamon!

SKILL

Ever wonder why we roast grains? Roasting brings out the very best in a grain by deepening its flavour. Either dry in a pan, with butter or oil, or even in the oven, roasting reduces the moisture in grains, brings out a nice nutty flavour, and makes them less 'sticky'.

Oh! Don't forget to keep stirring while roasting, to make sure every grain is equally roasted.

LUNCH OR NOT TO LUNCH?

1. SPICY SRIRACHA PRAWN WRAP   66

2. CHICKEN KATHI ROLLS   68

3. MEDITERRANEAN GRILLED VEG WITH CREAM CHEESE ROLLS   72

4. MASON JAR MEALS   74

5. COUSCOUS, HALLOUMI, AND CHICKPEA SALAD   78

6. MAC AND MUSHROOM SOUP   79

7. EASY-PEASY BROCCOLI SOUP   80

8. CREAMY PRAWN AND WALNUT JAFFLE   82

9. COCONUT RICE WITH SAUTÉED GREEN CHUTNEY VEGETABLES   84

10. ROASTED SWEET POTATO, PINE NUTS, AND KALE SALAD
    WITH ORANGE HONEY DRESSING   86

LUNCH OR NOT TO LUNCH?

**At your desk or in the car,
these lunch ideas are mess-free and simple.**

Oh no, it's 12.30 p.m.

I've got just half an hour to drive to the meeting, and the journey usually takes sixty minutes.

My phone's buzzing. It's my colleague, who gets a panic attack every time I step out for a meeting. It's not like I'm having a romantic lunch date with George Clooney. Alas.

I'm starving. As I drive, I run the meeting's agenda through my head, something I always do. It's like a mental mini-rehearsal, right from the opening greeting. Argh, these hunger cramps are driving me nuts. Now, I can truly say I'm hangry (a mood you just wouldn't want to see me in).

I'm irritable and edgy and suddenly the meeting screenplay in my head is dimming.

I see a huge McD sign on the road. I turn in, order the cheapest burger on the menu, drum my fingers on the wheel while I wait for my burger.

What's the time? Oh no no no, it's 12.55! It's almost time and here I am with a burger in my hand—park and gobble or drive and eat? I look at my watch again. Drive and eat it is.

With each bite I can feel my senses returning, along with a tad bit of guilt that I had to resort to a takeout burger. I finally make it and as I step out, taking my final bite, a sneaky little mayo drip falls in slow motion and lands on the lapel of my black suit. A tissue pat and a few deep breaths and I make my way to the office building in my self-designed Dalmatian suit.

An hour later I sit in the car and smile into the rear view mirror, thinking I'm such a star, and just then I see there's green lettuce stuck between my teeth. Yikes!

Sound familiar? This version and many variations were the realities of my every day until I discovered some super cool, simple, and easy lunch ideas I could pack up or prepare on the weekend too. No mess and all so straightforward, these recipes can be prepped the previous day or in the morning if you have the ingredients already chopped. I usually slice

and dice enough for a few days and portion
them out for my meals.

Pick one of these recipes, whichever suits you,
on a day you know you'll be at your desk or on
the move. Whatever you're doing it's always a yes
to lunch because that's what gets you to rock
the second half of your day.

SPICY SRIRACHA PRAWN WRAP

INGREDIENTS

For the wraps

50 grams dried vermicelli noodles

4 rice wraps

5 or 6 iceberg, butter, or romaine lettuce leaves

1 spring onion, cut lengthwise into strips

½ red bell pepper, cut lengthwise into strips

4 or 5 mint leaves (optional), rinsed

5 or 6 fresh coriander sprigs, rinsed

For the shrimp

12 medium shrimp, deveined and washed

1 garlic clove, minced

½ tablespoon honey

½ lime, juice squeezed

1 tablespoon sriracha sauce

Salt

Freshly ground black pepper

Olive oil

Crunchy spicy prawns in a cold wrap with refreshing crisp lettuce and mint is a perfect, easy-to-make and fulfilling lunch.

What I particularly like about this recipe is its simplicity that still keeps the fire and zing quotient alive.

And—here's the best part—use rice paper wraps, tortilla wraps, or a day-old chapati (Indian flatbread) and just get rolling.

These rolls can be prepared a night ahead too. They store perfectly well overnight and are best eaten either slightly chilled or at room temperature.

Run a knife down the upper side of the shrimp where you see the dark vein, and peel it out.

SKILL

Rolls using wraps such as rice wraps can get dry pretty easily. The trick to keeping them from drying out is to **moisten a muslin cloth or a clean handkerchief,** squeeze out the excess water, if any, and place it over the rolled wraps.

I suggest doing the same for packed lunches as well before closing the lid.

SERVING

Makes: **4 wraps**

METHOD

1. Place the vermicelli noodles in a large bowl and fill it with boiling water. Wait for 2 minutes or till the noodles soften and strain (or follow the package instructions). Rinse immediately with tap water and set aside.

2. Preparing the shrimp: In a separate bowl, combine the garlic, honey, lime juice, and sriracha and season with salt and pepper. Mix well. Dip each shrimp into the marinade until they are all well coated.

3. In a shallow frying pan on low heat (or better still a grill pan), heat a little bit of olive oil. Add the shrimps and cook on each side for 2 to 3 minutes or until firm and opaque. Transfer the shrimps to a plate and set aside to cool. Drain the residual juices into a bowl and set aside.

4. If using rice paper, take a wide plate with high edges and pour some warm water into it. Place each sheet in the water until it softens, then remove immediately. If using a tortilla or chapati, simply warm for a few minutes in a skillet.

5. Preparing the wrap: Take one wrap and in the centre of the wrap, place 1 lettuce leaf. Top the lettuce leaf with a big pinch of vermicelli noodles, followed by 3 shrimps, a pinch of spring onion strips, a pinch of bell pepper strips, 1 mint leaf (if using), and 1 coriander sprig. Fold the bottom half over the filling. Fold the sides inwards and over, then roll to close the wrap. Repeat to make the remaining wraps.

Sriracha Soy Dip recipe on page 147

CHICKEN KATHI ROLLS

SERVING

Makes:
2 or 3 Kathi rolls

When it comes to Indian street food, Kathi rolls are the real deal. These rolls originated from Kolkata but now are a famous street eat across India.

Rolled in thin parathas (a version of Indian flatbread) with egg, mint, coriander chutney, and many spicy variants of meat kebabs, chicken, paneer or egg, every bite is a burst of Indian spice and cool chutney.

These are great as starters if you have guests; just slice up your roll and in no time, it's a swipe! My favourite filling is chicken because it's quick, and most times I use leftover grilled chicken for this recipe.

Sip a fresh fruit juice on the side, peeps, because it can get a little hot! For a vegetarian version, simply replace the chicken with crumbled cottage cheese.

INGREDIENTS

2 medium boneless chicken breasts

Salt

Freshly ground black pepper

1 teaspoon white vinegar

4 egg whites

1 tablespoon coriander leaves, finely chopped

Olive oil

2 frozen parathas

½ medium onion, finely sliced

½ green bell pepper, finely sliced

1 small tomato, finely sliced

Pinch ground turmeric

Pinch red chilli powder or ground paprika

2 tablespoons green chutney (page 148)

2 big pinches finely sliced onion

Handful grated white cheddar or mozzarella cheese (optional)

METHOD

1. Place a saucepan on medium heat. Add the chicken breasts and just enough water to cover them. Add a pinch of salt and pepper and the vinegar. Bring to a boil and allow the chicken to cook for 5 minutes or until the meat is white and slightly soft when you press it. Drain the water and set the chicken aside. Once cooled, cut the chicken breast into thin strips.

2. Beat the egg whites in a bowl along with the coriander leaves. Season with salt and pepper.

3. Place a shallow frying pan on low heat. Add a little olive oil and when it is slightly heated, pour half the egg mixture into the pan, swirling the egg until there is a really thin, even layer in the pan. Fry the egg on both sides, remove from the pan, and set aside. Repeat with the remaining egg white mixture.

4. In a frying pan, <u>heat up the frozen parathas</u> until soft and slightly crispy. Set aside to cool.

Keep them frozen until you cook them.

5. Place the frying pan back on medium heat with a tablespoon of oil. Once the oil is slightly heated, add the sliced onion, bell pepper, and tomato, and fry for a few minutes until slightly softened. Add the chicken, turmeric, and chilli powder. You can add a few splashes of water, if required, to help stir-fry the ingredients. Cook until there is no moisture in the pan and the mixture is dry. Check for seasoning, turn the heat off, and leave to cool before serving.

6. Let's roll:

   a. In the middle of one paratha, spread half the green chutney, making sure you don't take it all the way to the edges.

   b. Place one fried egg on top ("tear" just enough to layer the paratha)

   c. Take a spoonful of chicken mixture and pack it tightly lengthwise in the centre of the paratha.

   d. Finish with a few slices of onion and grated white cheese (if using). Roll the parathas while keeping the filling tightly packed.

   e. Repeat to make the remaining rolls.

SKILL

Don't be overwhelmed by the number of steps in this recipe. Take a breath and look at it: It's basically four main steps:

1) **The fried egg**
2) **The chicken mixture**
3) **Warming the parathas**
4) **Rolling**

When you break it down like this, you'll see it's a real simple recipe to whip up. Remember to get the ingredients ready before you start cooking, and you're set.

Green coriander
and mint chutney
(see page 148)

MEDITERRANEAN GRILLED VEG WITH CREAM CHEESE ROLLS

Makes:
2 or 3 wraps

Colourful, crunchy, and cheesy, three Cs that will make any meat-eater want to dive into one of my favourite vegetarian wraps. And honestly, can it possibly go wrong if it's teamed with cream cheese?

That was my extra touch one day when I felt the wrap needed some oomph, and a generous spread of cream cheese did the trick. Served warm or cold, this wrap tastes equally good either way.

If you're packing the wrap for later in the day or preparing it the previous night, here's a tip: Leave the cream cheese out to avoid a soggy wrap!

Instead, make a dip for your wrap: Combine half a crushed garlic clove, a generous sprinkle of paprika, a pinch of salt, and some chopped chives or green tips from the spring onion. Mix well with the cream cheese. Dip the wrap before every bite.

INGREDIENTS

3 inches courgette, cut into thick strips lengthwise

¼ red bell pepper, cut into thick strips lengthwise

¼ yellow bell pepper, cut into thick strips lengthwise

4 fresh mushrooms, cut into quarters

1 medium onion, cut into big chunks (cut in half and then into three parts)

2 garlic cloves, peeled

2 tablespoons extra-virgin olive oil

2 teaspoons balsamic vinegar

Pinch each of dry herbs, such as rosemary, thyme, oregano

Salt

Freshly ground black pepper

2 tortilla wraps

3 tablespoons cream cheese, at room temperature

2 lettuce leaves

METHOD

1. Preheat the oven to 210°C.

2. In a deep bowl, combine the courgette, bell peppers, mushrooms, onion, garlic, olive oil, vinegar, and herbs. Season well with salt and pepper. Mix well until all the vegetables are well coated, then transfer them to a grilling pan.

3. Place the pan in the preheated oven and roast the vegetables for 10 to 12 minutes or until they begin to shrivel and their edges brown slightly. Remove the pan from the oven and set aside.

4. Let's roll:

   a. Take one tortilla wrap and warm it slightly in a skillet over medium heat.

   b. When cooled, spread it with half the cream cheese, leaving the edges clear.

   c. Place a lettuce leaf in the centre. Then lay half the grilled vegetables on top.

   d. Roll the tortilla wrap over the filling while keeping the filling tightly packed. You can wrap one end with aluminium foil for an easy hold.

   e. Repeat to make the remaining rolls.

5. Serve the rolls at room temperature or chilled.

SKILL

When grilling vegetables, **it's important to understand the kind of vegetables you pair together and why.**

Yellow and red bell peppers add sweetness to the mix, mushrooms give a meaty texture, and courgettes adds to the crunch. They also cook at relatively the same pace.

Carrots and beans, though great, have longer cooking times and aren't ideal for quick vegetable grills.

MASON JAR MEALS

SERVING

Makes:
**1 (approximately
1-L) tall mason jar**

Mason jar meals are super easy and convenient. Stack the ingredients, and when you're ready to eat, all you need to do is pour some hot water into the jar or simply dive your fork into that salad.

Yes, totally possible to get some flavour cravings satisfied during work hours. Mason jars can be prepared the night before. They make great leftovers for the next meal too. And if your colleague hovers around your desk, don't blame me.

Don't forget to Instagram your mason jar meals—they make great food pics for your friends to envy. Plus, now you have time to whip up some dessert!

METHOD

1. Layer the ingredients in the mason jar in the order listed.

2. When ready to eat, pour just enough boiling water into the jar to cover the ingredients by ½ inch.

3. Close the jar and leave for 15 to 20 minutes before serving.

Stand back and watch the magic happen.

Ever wonder why we roast grains?

SKILL

Roasting brings out the very best in a grain by **deepening its flavour.** Either dry in a pan, with butter or oil, or even in the oven, roasting reduces the moisture in grains, brings out a nice nutty flavour, and makes them less 'sticky'.

Oh! Don't forget to **keep stirring while roasting,** to make sure every grain is equally roasted.

INGREDIENTS

Tom Yum	**Beef Ramen Noodles**
1 tablespoon Tom Yum soup paste	**1** beef stock cube, crumbled
½ tablespoon soy sauce	**8 to 10 drops** sesame oil
1 lime, juice squeezed	**2 teaspoons** soy sauce
Pinch sugar	**½ cup** carrot, shredded
1 tablespoon fresh ginger, thickly sliced	**8** button mushrooms, thinly sliced
1 (4-inch) piece lemongrass, sliced diagonally	**150 grams** thinly sliced cooked beef steak
3 button mushrooms, chopped	**Handful** baby spinach leaves, finely sliced
½ cup red bell pepper, chopped	**Handful** spring onions, finely chopped
3 or 4 cooked medium shrimp (frozen or fresh, boil in salted water until pink and firm)	**1 packet (about 100 grams)** dried ramen noodles
2 tablespoons spring onions, finely chopped	**2 or 3** red chillies, finely chopped
Handful mung bean sprouts	
½ cup fresh coriander with stems, roughly chopped	
1 red chilli, finely sliced	

Tom Yum

Beef
Ramen Noodles

COUSCOUS, HALLOUMI, AND CHICKPEA SALAD

INGREDIENTS

½ teaspoon za'atar

1 tablespoon olive oil

150 grams Halloumi cheese, cut into small cubes

½ cup couscous

¼ cup raisins

1 cup boiling water

2 tablespoons extra-virgin olive oil

2 tablespoons lemon juice, freshly squeezed

1 garlic clove, minced

1 teaspoon ground cumin

1 teaspoon ground coriander

Salt

½ red bell pepper, finely chopped

1 spring onion, finely chopped

Handful canned chickpeas, rinsed and drained

8 to 10 parsley sprigs, finely chopped

Freshly ground black pepper

This salad makes me happy. It's colourful, zesty, sweet, and aromatic.

It is perfect on its own, or try it as a side salad with baked fish, chicken or meat.

Not a fan of raisins? You can use pomegranate seeds instead.

SKILL

Halloumi cheese has a **high melting point and is semi-hard,** which makes it great for grilling.

It's kept in brine and is usually salty, so **always check the cheese** before adding any additional seasoning.

You can use the same mix of za'atar and olive oil to make **Halloumi fries** too.

SERVING

Serves: **1**

METHOD

1. Mix the za'atar and olive oil well in a bowl. Add the Halloumi cheese and mix well.

2. Place a frying pan on low heat. When the pan is slightly warm, fry the marinated Halloumi cheese until the sides are golden brown. Set aside to cool.

3. Mix the couscous with the raisins in a glass bowl and pour in the boiling water. Cover the bowl with a plate to contain the steam and let sit for 5 minutes.

4. Meanwhile, in a small bowl, combine the oil, lemon juice, garlic, cumin and coriander. Season with salt and pepper; whisk well.

5. Uncover the bowl containing the couscous, and with a fork, separate or fluff the couscous grains. Stir in the bell pepper, spring onion, chickpeas, and parsley. Add the Halloumi cheese cubes.

6. Pour the dressing over the salad and toss together until well mixed.

MAC AND MUSHROOM SOUP

SERVING

Serves: **2**

INGREDIENTS

½ cup macaroni

250 grams fresh button mushrooms (white or brown), roughly chopped

Salt

Knob butter

½ small onion, roughly chopped

2 garlic cloves, crushed

2 cups water

2 tablespoons cooking cream

Freshly ground black pepper

Sometimes, a bowl of fresh creamy mushroom soup is all that's needed to unwind.

I like to throw in some macaroni to make it more wholesome and filling. With or without the macaroni, this soup is really simple and is included in this book because I get more requests for this soup than any other recipe.

Short on time? Lose the macaroni. Want to keep it light? Lose the cream. Play with your recipes and make them yours!

METHOD

1. Pour about 1 cup of water into a saucepan on medium heat. When the water begins to boil, add in the macaroni with a pinch of salt. Cook the macaroni until it's still slightly firm (what the Italians call 'al dente'). Remove from the heat and drain.

2. Wash the mushrooms and set aside.

3. Place a pan on low heat and melt the butter. Once melted, add the onion and garlic and stir for a few minutes until the onion is translucent.

4. Add the chopped mushrooms and sauté until softened. Add the water and bring it to a simmer. Season with salt. Remove the pan from the heat and let the mixture cool slightly.

5. Transfer the contents to a blender. Blend the mix to a smooth consistency.

6. Pour the soup into a serving bowl and stir in the cooking cream.

7. Mix in the cooked macaroni and finish with some freshly ground pepper.

SKILL

Try using a **mix of mushrooms** like shiitake, oyster, porcini, portobello, and enoki.

That's a wild mushroom soup right there with deep rich mushroom flavours, not to mention nutritionally rich too.

EASY-PEASY BROCCOLI SOUP

SERVING

Serves: **2**

INGREDIENTS

2 cups water

Salt

150 to 200 grams broccoli florets

4 or 5 coriander sprigs

1 teaspoon grated Parmesan cheese

Freshly ground black pepper

Select the brightest green ones!

A simple fresh bowl of soup does wonders. The best part about this recipe is that it's versatile. You can throw in most vegetables.

My top pick is broccoli but I've also tried this with pumpkin (yum!), celery, and carrot. When I've got a big head of broccoli I happily divide half for a good 'ol bowl of hot steaming soup.

Mom made a few tweaks by adding coriander sprigs to the recipe to keep it flavourful but still light, simple, and quick.

METHOD

1. Put the water in a saucepan to boil with a generous sprinkle of salt.

2. Add the broccoli florets to the pan and allow to cook for about 5 to 7 minutes. To check if the broccoli is cooked, scoop a floret to the side of the pan; if it breaks easily, that's a sign to turn off the heat. Stir in the coriander sprigs.

3. When slightly cooled, pour the contents into a blender. Blend the mix to a smooth consistency.

4. Reheat the soup just before serving, and taste to check the seasoning. Serve with the grated Parmesan cheese and freshly ground pepper.

SKILL

To keep the soup atomic green, **don't cover the broccoli while it's boiling.** Also, add the coriander at the very end; herbs don't require cooking anyway.

This way your key ingredients stay bright green and so does the soup when blended.

CREAMY PRAWN AND WALNUT JAFFLE

INGREDIENTS

3 walnuts, soaked in water for at least 20 to 30 minutes and then finely chopped

6 medium prawns, preboiled with a pinch of salt and then finely chopped

3 tablespoons cream cheese

3 inches cucumber, peeled and shredded

1 or 2 spring onions, finely chopped

Ground paprika

Salt

Freshly ground black pepper

½ lime, juice squeezed

4 slices white bread

Shredded mozzarella

Butter, at room temperature

The first time I heard the term _jaffle_ was when I visited Sydney, Australia for my cousin's wedding.

The Aussies are great at creating cool-sounding lingo, and jaffle is simply an iron-grilled toasted sandwich. Ha! Jaffles are best just off the grill, but if you can't eat them straight away, they pack well for office or late lunches.

The sandwich maker almost pressure-seals the sides of the sandwiches, locking in the flavours. From sweet to savoury stuffing, you can jaffle just about anything. I love biting into the crunchiness of the prawn and walnut and melted cheese of this jaffle. Hmm, I think I'll make one right now!

SERVING

Makes: **2 jaffles**

METHOD

1. Preheat the sandwich maker.

2. Combine the walnuts, prawns, cream cheese, cucumber, and spring onions in a bowl. Season well with paprika, salt, and pepper, then add the lime juice. Mix well to create a creamy sandwich stuffing mix.

3. On one slice of bread, spread a generous amount of the sandwich mix.

4. Take some mozzarella cheese and spread it over the sandwich mix. Cover with the second bread slice and butter the top side.

5. Repeat steps 3 and 4 to make the second sandwich.

6. Brush a little butter on the plates of the preheated sandwich maker. Immediately place the sandwiches on the plates and close the lid. Grill for about 5 minutes or until the sandwiches are toasted with a nice golden-brown crisp surface. Cut the jaffles in half and serve while still hot.

SKILL

If you don't have a sandwich maker, you can make the same jaffle **in a skillet.** Yes! Place the sandwiches on a hot skillet and lay a metal lid on top of them. Put a weight on the lid to create some pressure. Same effect, same taste.

Don't let this recipe pass you by. Improvise!

Load it, baby! You can never have enough cheese in a sandwich :

COCONUT RICE WITH SAUTÉED GREEN CHUTNEY VEGETABLES

SERVING

Serves: **2**

Coconut rice is one of my top go-to comfort foods. I love coconut-anything.

The aroma, coolness, and calm flavours of this dish make it an excellent pairing with spicy or relatively stronger flavours, such as green chutney vegetables.

Green chutney is a flavour bomb with mint, coriander, ginger, lime, and chillies. It's true when they say you eat with your eyes first, and this recipe, with its vibrant white and green colours, is a testimony to that. Garnish the rice with fried onions, and serve with some mango pickle and poppadoms.

Now you know how to impress your vegetarian or vegan friends too.

INGREDIENTS

For the rice

1 teaspoon coconut oil

2 green cardamom pods

1 inch cinnamon stick

3 cloves

½ cup white basmati rice, soaked in water

½ cup coconut milk

½ cup lukewarm water

Salt

For the vegetables

Coconut or olive oil

1 cup mixed vegetables (use a mix of bell peppers, broccoli, courgettes, and button mushrooms) chopped to a uniform medium-size

Salt

Freshly ground black pepper

2 tablespoons green chutney (page 148)

METHOD

To make the rice

1. Heat the coconut oil on low heat in a deep pot. When slightly warm, add the cardamom, cinnamon, and cloves. Stir until the spices turn aromatic.

2. Strain the rice and add it to the pot. Stir for a few minutes before adding the coconut milk and lukewarm water. Season with salt. Raise the heat to high and cover the pot with a tightly fitting lid for 3 to 4 minutes or until you see holes on the top surface of the rice (this means the water has almost evaporated). Turn the heat down immediately and place the pot on a skillet and set the skillet on low heat. Let the rice continue to cook for 10 to 15 minutes, without lifting the lid.

3. Once done, while still warm, fluff the rice with a fork.

To make the vegetables

1. While the rice is cooking, place a frying pan on high heat. Pour in a bit of oil and when it is warm, add the mixed vegetables. Season with salt and pepper and, still maintaining the high heat, sauté the vegetables, tossing them every few minutes.

2. When the mushrooms begin to soften and the vegetables begin to get subtle brown tones, stir in the green chutney. Add a splash of water and let the moisture evaporate. When the vegetables are thickly coated with chutney, turn off the heat and set the pan aside.

Cooking rice takes practice and attention. But, trust me, once you get the knack of it, your confidence will know no bounds. Just follow the instructions in this recipe and you're all set.

Cooking rice has a few rules:

a) The grain to water ratio is always 1:2 (i.e., ½ cup rice and 1 cup water).

b) Cook first on high heat until you see the holes (like craters) in the surface of the rice.

c) Immediately lower the heat and place the pan on a skillet. This avoids the rice burning from the bottom.

d) After you turn the heat off, do not open the lid until the time of serving.

Glass lids are best for cooking rice because you can see the holes without lifting the lid. If you don't have a glass lid, feel free to open the lid once or twice to check.

ROASTED SWEET POTATO, PINE NUTS, AND KALE SALAD WITH ORANGE HONEY DRESSING

INGREDIENTS

250 grams sweet potatoes, peeled and cut into ½-inch cubes

Salt

Freshly ground black pepper

1 to 1½ tablespoons butter, melted

3 tablespoons pine nuts

¼ cup unsweetened fresh orange juice

1 small lime, juice squeezed

2 tablespoons extra-virgin olive oil

1 tablespoon honey

2 cups kale leaves, finely chopped

Handful freshly grated Parmesan cheese

I always found salads boring. After all, what's in them? Some torn green leaves, raw veggies, nuts, maybe? And some sour dressing.

Sadly, that was my interpretation of salad and so for many, many years I avoided them like the plague. Until the time I was invited to a formal sit-down dinner, and yes, the first course was salad. I mentally rolled my eyes and tried to act all civilised.

Dug my fork into crunchy leaves tossed with green apple (apple?!) and into my mouth, setting off fireworks in my head. The flavours were made for each other and now, I can't get enough of salads. Not only are they quick, they're guilt-free, satisfying, and fireworks-in-your-head worthy! This salad is one of my favourites because of the textures and flavours from the roasted sweet potato, nuttiness of the pine nuts, earthiness of the dark green crunchy kale, and zing of the sweet citrus dressing.

Don't have kale? Use any salad leaf in your fridge. Improvise. But don't give your salad a pass for takeout. I'm watching you. ☺

SERVING

Makes: **1 standard salad bowl**

METHOD

1. Preheat the oven to 200°C.

2. On a baking tray, season the sweet potato cubes with salt and pepper and mix well with the melted butter. Bake the sweet potatoes for about 20 minutes or until the cubes turn slightly brown and caramelized. Once done, remove the tray from the oven and set aside.

3. In a small pan on low heat, toast the pine nuts until fragrant and lightly golden brown. Remove from the heat and set aside.

4. Making the dressing: In a small bowl, whisk the orange juice, lime juice, olive oil, and honey, and season with 1 teaspoon of pepper and a pinch of salt. Set aside.

5. In a bowl, combine the kale leaves, toasted pine nuts, and sweet potato (cooled or at room temperature). Drizzle the dressing over the salad and toss well. Taste and adjust the seasoning, if necessary.

6. Top with the grated Parmesan cheese and serve fresh.

Be generous now.

SASS!

When a recipe requires some ingredients to be precooked or heated and then cooled, **always start with the warmest ingredients,** which may take a longer time to cool down.

This way, when you bring all the ingredients together, everything is at room temperature and you can whip up your dish quickly instead of twiddling your thumbs waiting for the sweet potatoes or pine nuts, in this case, to cool down.

Work smart, not hard!

BEFORE DINNER MUNCHIES

1.	TURMERIC AND HONEY KALE CRISPS	94
2.	REEJ'S ALMOND BREAD	96
3.	PAN CON TOMATE	98
4.	VANILLA KAAPI LASSI	100
5.	SHAKKAR ROTI	102
6.	BACON-WRAPPED GOAT'S CHEESE-STUFFED DATES	104
7.	BUTTER AND HERB SAUTÉED MUSHROOMS WITH DILL AND GARLIC DIP	106
8.	DARK CHOCOLATE AND ROASTED ALMOND NUT BUTTER	108
9.	BOMBAY SANDWICH	110

BEFORE DINNER MUNCHIES

**Those small bites that
keep you going.**

If I'm still at work a few hours post lunchtime,
I'm usually checking my drawers for half-eaten
chocolate bars. If I'm at home plonked on the
sofa, I'm the Cookie Monster. It's the 4 p.m.-
ish to 7 p.m.-ish window when lunch is well
digested and it's too early to eat dinner that
the before-dinner cravings kick in. I remember
the days when my office drawer was filled with
Snickers, salted nuts, and dark chocolate–coated
rice crackers. Done with one and within thirty
minutes I was craving another.

Nutritionally, I knew what was happening, but
timewise it was my best bet . . . until the day I
started experimenting with creating super easy
snacks. And now I'm a happy bunny. I still have
the occasional Snickers, but it's more of a treat
than a quick fix.

Here's the cool bit: Some of these recipes make
fantastic starters for a more fancy dinner, too! So
no sweating over 'what's for starters?' if you're
throwing a party. The best part is recipes like

Pan Con Tomate can be a fun DIY activity with guests. It doesn't stop there—I've actually been known to eat the Almond Bread for breakfast on really hungry days. Don't judge me!

Here are just a few ideas, but really what I'd love is for you to get the hang of the basics and feel empowered to improvise yourself. Find out what works for you, with what you've got left in the fridge. Maybe you're someone who likes taking some time out to prepare a snack, or maybe you need something that can be assembled in under half a minute, tops.

—

WITH A LITTLE PRACTICE AND CARE, COOKING FOR YOURSELF WILL BECOME AN EASY HABIT YOU WILL LOVE.

—

TURMERIC AND HONEY KALE CRISPS

INGREDIENTS

3 or 4 kale leaves, stems on (roughly 2 handfuls torn leaves)

½ tablespoon extra-virgin olive oil

½ teaspoon onion powder

½ teaspoon ground paprika

½ teaspoon honey

Pinch ground turmeric

Pinch sea salt

When something is crunchy yet healthy, I'm doing the happy dance in my head.

Do you remember when everyone was all about kale? Kale salads, kale soups, kale smoothies, and even kale *body scrubs?!* I was in the zone where the next person who mentioned kale would see me flinging a bunch straight at them.

However, I must admit that this curly-wurly dark green leaf has been stress-tested and is here to stay. Here's something fun I do: make a bowl of microwave popcorn, crunch some of these kale crisps, and toss it! Now I have a guilt-free snack to eat while I watch some Netflix.

I love this part; it's like giving a baby a good massage!

METHOD

1. Wash the kale leaves thoroughly (with the stems on), shake them well to discard the water drops, and lay them flat on paper towels. Now cover them with another layer of paper towels, sandwiching the kale leaves to remove the maximum amount of moisture.

2. Preheat the oven to 120°C. Line a baking tray with parchment paper.

3. Combine the oil, onion powder, paprika, honey, turmeric, and salt in a large bowl and mix well until it becomes a semi-solid reddish paste.

4. Working with one kale leaf at a time, use a fresh paper towel to fully wipe down the leaf, removing as much moisture as possible. This is an important step so don't rush your way through it. Now, tear the leaf from the main stem into medium pieces. Add the torn kale leaves to the olive oil mix, making sure you massage each piece until all the leaves are well marinated with the paste. You'll know you've done this right when the leaves are dark green and shiny.

5. Spread out the kale on the baking tray in a single layer, making sure not to crowd the tray.

6. Place the tray in the oven and bake for 13 to 15 minutes, checking occasionally. The kale leaves should begin to shrivel around the edges, turn dark green, and become crispy, but not brown, so keep an eye out for that.

7. Remove from the oven when done and set aside to cool for 2 to 3 minutes.

SASS!

While you wait for the kale crisps to get done, **try this face mask** using two ingredients from the list: mix ¼ teaspoon of ground turmeric with 1 teaspoon of honey.

Apply it in one thick layer over your face and keep it on until you feel the mask tighten over your skin. Rinse and pat dry. Now you can enjoy your freshly baked kale crisps with **glowing skin** too!

REEJ'S ALMOND BREAD

SERVING

Serves: **1**

INGREDIENTS

2 heaped tablespoons almond flour

1 tablespoon butter, melted

½ teaspoon baking powder

1 egg

Pinch ground cinnamon

Pinch ground nutmeg

1 teaspoon honey

2 teaspoons peanut butter

My friend Reeja would give any fashionista a run for her money and is younger than a teen at heart.

Even though we're more than a generation apart, we can talk for hours about food, life, spirituality and anything under the sun. She's a real pal and from sharing new ideas, fitness or even fashion tips, we're always cheering each other on, living our best lives yet.

She shared this recipe one day on WhatsApp: "Hey, check this out—almond bread in the microwave! Sorts out my midday cravings while on paleo." To which I responded, "Paleo? I thought we were doing keto." Thanks, Reej!

METHOD

1. Combine all the ingredients in a large mug and whisk well to get a thick, smooth batter.

2. Place the mug in the microwave for 90 seconds.

3. Allow the mug to cool down for 1 minute and overturn the mug. The bread will slide out smoothly.

4. Slice the bread and enjoy it with butter or as is.

SKILL

Before adding any ingredients to the mug, dip your fingers into the melted butter when it's slightly cool and **rub the insides of the mug;** this helps the bread slide out more easily, leaving no crumbs.

PAN CON TOMATE

SERVING

Serves: **1**

INGREDIENTS

2 large slices
rustic or any
artisan bread
(such as German
rye or sourdough),
medium thickness

Extra-virgin
olive oil

1 medium tomato,
rinsed

Crushed sea salt
or coarsely
ground salt

2 garlic cloves,
peeled and
crushed

This little piece of toasted bread with freshly grated tomato paste, crushed garlic, extra-virgin olive oil, and sea salt is a taste explosion in every bite.

When I first arrived for graduate study in Madrid, I used to stroll down the streets watching Spaniards relishing *pan con tomate* as one of their most-loved tapas. Eventually I mastered the walk and talk of popping by the neighbourhood tapas bar and in an almost-right Spanish accent say, *"Uno pan con tomate y uno cortado, por favor"*.

I miss those days, but food can magically time travel your mind and connect you right back to memories.

Can something so simple taste so good? Check it out for yourself . . .

METHOD

1. Preheat the oven to 200°C.

2. Arrange the bread slices on a baking tray. Lightly brush some olive oil on both sides of the bread slices.

3. Place the tray in the oven for about 5 minutes on each side or until lightly toasted.

4. While the bread is toasting, cut the tomato in half and, using a grater over a bowl, grate the tomato. What you'll get is a coarse tomato paste. Discard the tomato skin. Add 1 teaspoon of olive oil and a pinch of salt. Mix well.

5. Rub the crushed garlic on the toasted bread slices. Using a spoon, carefully spread the tomato mixture onto the toasted bread slices. Finish off with a drizzle of olive oil and a sprinkle of coarsely ground salt.

It's easier to grate them in a circular motion, rather than up and down.

SASS! Have fun while cooking and set the mood: **Get a little loco** by moving those hips to "Bailando" by Enrique Iglesias as you prepare this recipe!

VANILLA KAAPI LASSI

Serves: **2**

INGREDIENTS

1 cup milk

⅓ cup Greek yoghurt

2 tablespoons honey

1 small scoop vanilla ice-cream

½ teaspoon ground cardamom

2 espresso shots or **200 ml** prepared strong coffee

Ice cubes

Lassi is a traditional yoghurt-based drink native to India and is usually had sweet or spiced, while Kaapi is the South-Indian phonetic of the word coffee in the local language.

The first time I heard the word *kaapi* was during a train journey in Kerala. We would visit our relatives every summer and I still have vivid memories of playing with my plaited hair while staring at the platform hawkers shouting, 'Kaapi, Kaapi' as the train came to a halt. Served in a small white paper cup, the coffee gave you a similar kick to a tequila shot!

And so, on warm afternoons when I crave a cool, sweet beverage with an espresso shot to get me through the second half of the day, I remember those childhood kaapis. For this recipe, I played around with a few ingredients, poured them into a blender, and took a sip.

Dare to try?

METHOD

1. Combine all the ingredients, except the coffee and ice cubes, in a blender and blitz well.

2. Fill two tall glasses with ice and divide the coffee equally between them. Pour the blitzed vanilla lassi over the ice, and enjoy!

SASS!

Quick recipes such as this earn you some time, so use it wisely. Think of a family member or friend you meant to get in touch with this week but didn't find the time. **Pick up the phone** or have a mini-WhatsApp conversation while sipping your vanilla kaapi lassi.

SHAKKAR ROTI

SERVING

Makes: **12 rotis**

Scrolling up my Instagram feed one day I came across a charming, cosy looking homestay nestled in the Tirthan Valley, in the Himalayan state of Himachal Pradesh, India.

The next thing I know I was on a plane and on my way to visit the Gone Fishing Cottages owned by Dimple and Uppi, who are all heart. From the picturesque pine forests and red bridge over the river (where I enjoyed sitting and dangling my legs over the rapids) to the food served there, it was pure magic. One evening Dimple asked me if I had ever tasted Shakkar Roti (Sweet Indian Bread in Hindi). I bit into what looked like a rather ordinary roti rolled up with some brown sugary stuffing, and believe me, I bit into a piece of heaven.

The taste of warm, soft palm sugar melted with ghee balanced with roti is one of my favourite recipes. I usually buy rotis from the local supermarket where I can find whole-wheat, brown, and fortified versions.

But if you feel like making some from scratch, here's the recipe straight from Gone Fishing Cottages. Thanks, Dimple!

INGREDIENTS

For the rotis

1 teaspoon olive oil, plus more for greasing the bowl

2½ cups all-purpose flour, plus **½ cup** for dusting the work surface

1 cup hot water

For the shakkar mix

4 tablespoons pure ghee, melted

5 tablespoons jaggery (palm sugar) powder

I like to experiment with coconut sugar too; it's divine.

I've seen my mom lay out wax or parchment paper dusted with flour. She then lays the discs on the newspaper and lines up the rotis before cooking them in the skillet.

METHOD

1. Grease your hands with a little olive oil and rub the inside of a deep-bottomed bowl (this prevents the dough sticking to the bowl while kneading). Pour 2.5 cups of flour into the bowl and make a hole in the centre with a finger. Pour 1 teaspoon of olive oil into the hole, then slowly add the hot water while gently mixing with a spoon. Use a spoon because the dough will be quite hot.

2. Using your hands, knead the dough until it is soft and pliable. This could take up to 5 minutes.

Really punch and poke the dough. It's a great stress buster.

3. Cover the bowl with a damp cloth or plastic wrap and let it rest for at least 15 to 30 minutes. This helps the gluten release, which makes the dough more elastic. Remove the cloth and knead the dough once again.

4. Prepare to roll out the rotis by dusting some flour onto the work surface. Portion the dough into small balls and roll it out into thin discs, 4 to 5 inches in diameter. You can use a plate with sharp edges to make perfect circles (simply flip the plate and use it as a roti cutter). Remove the excess dough from the sides, then remove the plate, and you have a perfect circle.

5. Put a skillet on low heat and place a disc in the skillet. Wait for tiny air bubbles to start appearing, then flip the roti. It could take 2 to 3 minutes until both sides are lightly brown. Continue until all the rotis are prepared.

6. Preparing the shakkar mix: Add the warm melted ghee to the jaggery powder and stir until well mixed and smooth.

7. Take one roti at a time and place it on a plate. Spread 1 to 2 teaspoons of the ghee-sugar mixture on the roti and roll it up. You can cover one end with aluminium foil to make it easy to hold.

SASS!

This is also a great recipe to serve as an after-meal sweet treat. **Roti dough stores well in the freezer**, so if you have unexpected guests, simply thaw some dough, make your ghee-sugar mix, and you're set to impress.

I like to play around with this recipe, adding some shredded fresh coconut or chopped nuts to the mixture at times. Remember, forget the rules and **make it yours.**

BACON-WRAPPED GOAT'S CHEESE-STUFFED DATES

SERVING

Serves: **2 (makes 10 stuffed dates)**

INGREDIENTS

10 brown dates, pitted (seeds removed)

40 grams goat's cheese, at room temperature

10 pork bacon strips

10 toothpicks

One of my favourite things about living in Dubai is its vibrant mix of cultures. For food enthusiasts, it's like going on a culinary journey every day.

I met Katherine as she and her family made Dubai their home for a few years and we quickly learnt food was our common love. One day Katherine invited me over to show her how to cook Indian biryani. In a cultural exchange of tastes, she said she would show me how to make bacon-wrapped goat's cheese–stuffed dates. My expression veered between 'ummm . . . err . . .' and 'oh my gosh, that sounds sooo . . . yum?'. But with some nudges and laughs, I tried it, and for a while, I think I prepared it almost every other night.

The combination of sweet and salty, creamy and crispy, warm from the oven is addictively delicious. These are perfect as entertainment starters. You can make this recipe well ahead and pop them into the oven when your friends begin to arrive. Thanks, Katherine!

METHOD

1. Preheat the oven to 180°C.

2. Lay the pitted dates across a baking tray.

3. Using a teaspoon, stuff the dates with the goat's cheese.

4. Take one date and wrap a bacon strip tightly around it, securing it with a toothpick. Repeat until you have wrapped all the dates.

5. Bake for 20 minutes or until the bacon is sizzling and crispy. When done, remove the tray and serve freshly baked!

SASS!

Looking at a pan that needs some scrubbing? Don't frown.

Simply add **a few drops of lemon essential oil and some hot water.** Leave the pan for one hour or overnight and watch it come sparkling clean when you scrub it (with minimal effort).

BUTTER AND HERB SAUTÉED MUSHROOMS WITH DILL AND GARLIC DIP

SERVING

Serves: **2**

INGREDIENTS

250 grams
fresh button
mushrooms

Knob butter

2 tablespoons
fresh parsley,
finely chopped

Salt

Freshly ground
black pepper

I enjoy anything mushroom, in any form: dried, fresh, tinned, and marinated.

While my family was shopping for souvenirs during a holiday in Singapore, I was busy scouting for different types of dried mushrooms in Chinatown.

It's no surprise that when I came across this version of stuffed mushrooms at a party, I couldn't stop popping them into my mouth. It's become one of my favourite go-to snacks.

I like using fresh mushrooms for this, but tinned works equally well. Serve with some homemade dill and garlic cream cheese dip . . . just so easy to whip up!

METHOD

1. Rinse the mushrooms to get the dirt off. Set aside.

2. Place a frying pan on low heat. Once the pan is heated, melt the butter; once frothy, add the mushrooms. Sauté until you see them change colour and soften. Remove from the heat.

3. Add the chopped parsley and season with salt and pepper. Toss or stir once, and serve warm as is or with the cream cheese dip.

Dill and garlic dip recipe on page 147

SASS!

Turn this dish into a **quick party snack:** Once the mushrooms have cooled, remove the stalks and stuff the mushroom cups with cream cheese dip. Easy and impressive.

DARK CHOCOLATE AND ROASTED ALMOND NUT BUTTER

SERVING

Makes:
1 (500-ml) jar

INGREDIENTS

Knob butter

100 grams dark chocolate, broken into chunks

250 grams almonds

2 tablespoons sunflower seeds

Pinch sea salt

**Did I mention I love nuts?
Like . . . I reallly love all thing nuts!**

When almond butter hit the food scene, I rushed to get some but stopped in my tracks when I saw the price tag. *What?!* I did what I do best, and that is read the ingredients and review the recipe in my head. How about if I add a block of 80 percent dark chocolate?

At home, I grabbed almonds from my pantry and roasted them, melted the chocolate, and poured it all into the food processor. What came out was something I kissed my fingers for.

METHOD

1. Preparing a double boiler: fill a saucepan with water slightly below the midway mark and place on medium heat. As you wait for the water to boil, combine the butter and chocolate in a fairly big glass bowl. Place the bowl on top of the saucepan (ensure the water doesn't touch the bottom of the bowl) and stir until the chocolate and butter are melted and completely smooth. Set aside.

2. Put a frying pan on low heat. Once the pan is hot, add in the almonds and roast them until they are aromatic and a shade darker. Remove from the heat and set aside.

3. In a food processor, combine the slightly cooled almonds and chocolate mixture. Add the sunflower seeds and salt. Process until a grainy but smooth butter forms (this can take a couple of minutes as the warmth and oils of the almonds begin to blend). Scoop the contents into a glass mason jar and store at room temperature.

SASS!

Ever considered maintaining a **creative or ideas journal in the kitchen?** Some of my best thoughts and ideas come while I'm in the kitchen or in the . . . shower!

So keep a journal handy and scribble down thoughts as they come.

Go nuts with this recipe... literally!
Try hazelnuts, cashews, Brazil nuts, or
even macadamia. Also, you can totally
skip the chocolate and butter step and
make pure nut butter instead.

BOMBAY SANDWICH

INGREDIENTS

1 small potato

Salt

Pinch ground cumin

Pinch ground cinnamon

Pinch ground coriander

Pinch dried mango powder (optional)

Pinch freshly ground black pepper

4 white bread slices

Butter, at room temperature

3 to 4 tablespoons green chutney (page 148)

1 small tomato, thinly sliced

1 small onion, thinly sliced

½ green bell pepper, thinly sliced

Cheese slices or shredded cheese

Street food is extremely popular in India, and people from all walks of life find their common ground at the food hawkers.

Every state has its must-try street food delicacy. The Bombay sandwich is Mumbai's pride (or Bombay, as it was known in yesteryear) and is popular for its freshly sliced vegetables layered with spicy coriander and mint chutney plus copious amounts of cheese, buttered and then grilled to perfection—it's a midday snack that even meat eaters crave.

When butter is needed for spreading, **make sure it's at room temperature.** Nothing worse than trying to spread cold butter.

Remember, get your ingredients to room temperature before you begin, to ensure equal cooking timings and ease of use.

SERVING

Serves: **2**

METHOD

1. Boil the potato with a pinch of salt until it becomes soft. Set aside to cool then peel and slice.

2. Making the sandwich spice mix: Combine the cumin, cinnamon, coriander, mango powder (if using), pinch of salt, and pepper and set aside.

3. Cut the crusts off the bread slices or leave them on, as preferred. Spread the butter evenly on one side of two slices, followed by some green chutney.

4. Layer the vegetables on top of the slices in this order: tomato, onion, bell pepper, potato.

5. Dust a generous pinch of sandwich spice mix on top of the layered vegetables.

6. Finally, finish with cheese before closing the sandwich with the remaining two bread slices. Spread a generous layer of butter on the top side.

7. Heat a sandwich maker and brush a little butter on the grill surface. Immediately, place the sandwiches carefully on the hot surface. Close and seal the maker and toast until the cheese has melted and the sandwich is golden brown. Serve hot.

EASY-PEASY-LEMON-SQUEEZY DINNERS

1. LOADED BROCCOLI AND POTATO BAKE — 118

2. CREAMY TOMATO MEAT LOVERS PASTA BAKE — 119

3. ROASTED GARLIC, CHILLI, AND SOY BAKED FISH — 122

4. INDIAN GRILLED CHICKEN WITH KACHUMBARETTE — 124

5. LEMONGRASS-INFUSED INDIAN COCONUT STEW — 126

6. MOM'S KHEEMA PAV — 128

7. AUNTY DIANA'S RED DAL — 130

8. EZRA'S EASY CHICKEN STIR FRY — 131

9. CHILLI PRAWNS IN LEMON AND GARLIC BUTTER — 132

10. WANNABE LEBANESE KOUSA — 134

11. SIMPLICIOUS EASY STEAK — 136

12. WATERMELON AND FETA CHEESE SALAD — 138

13. CABBAGE GYOZAS — 140

14. FRIED RICE BUDDHA BOWL — 142

EASY-PEASY-LEMON-SQUEEZY DINNERS

Heels on or hair worn high, these recipes are classics after a long day's work.

I walk in, drop my bag and keys on the side table, and head to the living room, and oh my, is that couch inviting. Just ten minutes, I convince myself. I plop myself horizontally, kick off my heels, loosen my hair, and take a deep breath.

The next thing I know, my phone's ringing, or the neighbours' kids are running around the corridor, or the laundry guy is ringing the doorbell, and I spring up in shock because the ten sweet minutes have turned into an hour. And just like that I reach for my phone and the next thing I know I've ordered my dinner through one of the many food delivery apps on my phone. Sigh.

If only I could get cracking in the kitchen and eat one hot meal made by myself end-to-end in thirty minutes—maybe even a quick fifteen minutes! So, after a few chats with Mom, countless hours online, and customizing recipes, trials and fails, I've found my go-to dinner list that's a success each and every time. Here are recipes you can get right into and get done in under thirty minutes.

Tried and tested and oh-so-good when you're curled up on the couch watching your favourite Netflix show with a plate of steaming hot food you've prepared yourself.

—

FRESH INGREDIENTS, SEASONED WITH A LITTLE LOVE AND CARE, YOU'LL WHIP UP DISHES THAT YOU'LL WANT TO SHARE.

—

LOADED BROCCOLI AND POTATO BAKE

INGREDIENTS

2 tablespoons butter, plus more for greasing the baking dish

1 large potato, boiled and cut into medium slices

½ small broccoli, cut into florets or sliced

100–150 grams beef salami or bacon, diced

1 large onion, cut into rings

½ teaspoon salt, plus more for seasoning layers

Freshly ground black pepper

2 tablespoons all-purpose flour

1½ cups milk, at room temperature

1 cup shredded white or yellow cheddar cheese

Breadcrumbs

Every Christmas, my sis-in-law Deepti prepares a winner of a baked potato dish.

Three years in a row and counting, we've had this creamy cheese potato bake and it has everyone going for seconds (and thirds). I've improvised a little to include broccoli because some part of me thinks I can sneak my greens in there and not feel so guilty about digging my fork time and again into this loaded bake. Thanks, Deeps!

SKILL

The trick to making good béchamel sauce lies in three things: **(1) Timing:** Keep the ingredients close at hand as one quickly follows the other; **(2) Temperature,** of both the ingredients (room temperature) and the dish on the heat (low to medium heat); and **(3) Patience:** Keep stirring so the flour and milk don't burn and the heat passes through evenly. As you pour in the milk, continue to whisk even after the cheese is added.

SERVING

Serves: **3 to 4 (makes one 9-by-13-inch baking dish)**

METHOD

1. Preheat the oven to 200°C.

2. Dot the baking dish with butter and spread it well.

3. Lay slices of potato to cover the bottom of the dish, followed with broccoli, salami, and onion. Season generously with salt and pepper. Repeat and complete another layer.

4. Place a pan on medium heat, and melt the butter. Once the butter starts to froth, mix in the flour and ½ teaspoon of salt, and stir constantly for a minute until a rubbery smooth mixture forms.

5. Using a whisk, pour in the milk slowly and whisk until the sauce has thickened. This could take a few minutes. Finally, stir in the cheese until it has melted. Check the seasoning and adjust the salt if necessary.

6. Pour the sauce over the layered ingredients in the baking dish, ensuring all the vegetables are evenly covered with the sauce.

7. Finish by sprinkling with the breadcrumbs and some extra cheddar cheese.

8. Bake for 20 minutes or until the top layer of breadcrumbs is golden brown and the cheese has melted.

CREAMY TOMATO MEAT LOVERS PASTA BAKE

INGREDIENTS

1½ cups penne pasta, or your favourite kind

Salt

Olive oil

100 grams turkey ham, diced

3 large garlic cloves, roughly chopped

2 heaped tablespoons fresh cream

½ cup milk

1 (400-gram) can diced tomatoes, with juices

Freshly ground black pepper

1 cup shredded cheese, such as mozzarella or a pasta cheese mix

100 grams sliced salami

½ cup shredded Parmesan cheese

1½ tablespoons cup dried herbs such as basil, thyme, rosemary, and oregano

Dried red chilli flakes

This recipe hails from my MBA days in Madrid. Between case study preps, assignment deadlines, laundry, and a growling tummy, I was forced to crack quick dishes.

The one-dish pasta bake worked like magic; I layered everything in the baking dish, topped it with dried herbs and a generous drizzle of olive oil, and voilà!

Twenty minutes and dinner was ready. Sometimes when you're racing against time, it brings out the best in you, at least in the kitchen!

SKILL

Peeling garlic cloves can be a pain.

Here's an easy way to do so: Cut the clove in half and then pinch it away from the skin. Garlic crushers are great, and the best part is that you can crush it along with the skin as only the minced part comes through.

SERVING

Serves: **2 (makes one 10.5-by-8-inch baking dish)**

METHOD

1. Preheat the oven to 200°C.

2. In a large saucepan, bring water to a boil, add the pasta, a big pinch of salt, and a generous drizzle of olive oil. Remove the pan from the heat when the pasta is only semi-cooked. Drain the pasta and set aside.

3. Lightly brush the sides and bottom of the baking dish with olive oil.

4. In a large bowl, mix the pasta with the turkey ham, garlic, cream, milk, and tomatoes, and season with salt and pepper. Stir in half the shredded cheese. Transfer the pasta mix to the baking dish and spread into an even layer.

5. Top the mixture with the salami, the remaining shredded cheese, and the Parmesan. Finish off by sprinkling with dried herbs, chilli flakes (as preferred) and generously drizzle with olive oil.

6. Bake for 20 to 25 minutes or until the top appears toasted and crispy.

7. Let cool for 5 to 10 minutes before serving.

Leftovers can be stored in an airtight container in the refrigerator for up to 3 days.

Creamy Tom
Meat Lover
Pasta Bak

Loaded Broccoli
and Potato
Bake

Sometimes when you're racing against time, it brings out the best in you, at least in the kitchen!

ROASTED GARLIC, CHILLI, AND SOY BAKED FISH

SERVING

Serves: **2**

INGREDIENTS

2 fresh white fish fillets

Salt

Freshly ground black pepper

6 tablespoons olive oil

2 teaspoons sesame seeds

2 spring onions, finely chopped

3 tablespoons soy sauce

1 to 1½ tablespoons fresh ginger, finely chopped

10 garlic cloves, finely chopped

2 tablespoons red chilli, finely chopped *(you can use a pinch of dried red chilli flakes as an alternative, or as much as you want to turn up the heat)*

I'll be honest here—I'm not a very big fan of fish. It's true and now I've said it out loud for the world to know.

Back in the days when I interned at hotels, I didn't get away that easily when I expressed my feelings about fish to chefs. In one such instance, a chef said "WAIT! I'm going to prepare a baked fish, and you will taste it and let me know what you think."

As he set a plate before me, the aromas of roasted garlic, ginger, chilli, and soy were so enticing I devoured the entire fillet. So, if you feel the same way about fish as I did, try this and see for yourself.

You can try this recipe with **any fish or shellfish,** so if you love your seafood, then do try it with shrimp, crab, salmon, and lobster.

To check if fish is cooked, pierce it with a fork; if the fork passes through smoothly and the fish flakes, it's done.

METHOD

1. Preheat the oven to 190°C and line a baking tray with two sheets of aluminium foil side by side. The foil sheets should be big enough to wrap the fish fillets.

2. Place one fish fillet in the middle of each foil sheet. Season the fish with salt and pepper on both sides.

3. In a glass bowl, combine the olive oil, sesame seeds, spring onions, soy sauce, ginger, garlic, and chilli and mix thoroughly.

4. Using your hands, gently coat both sides of the fish fillets with the marinade.

5. Bring the two ends of one foil sheet together (forming a tent) and roll them downwards towards the fillet. Stop halfway and seal the gaps on either side by pinching them together so that the marinade cannot escape. Repeat the wrapping process with the second fillet.

6. Bake the fish for 25 minutes. Remove the baking tray from the oven and carefully open the top edges of the foil sheets so the fish fillets are fully exposed. Return the tray to the oven for a further 10 minutes. This is where the roasting of the garlic and final baking takes place.

7. Once done, rest the fillets on the tray for 5 minutes. This dish is wonderful served with some steamed rice or a side salad.

INDIAN GRILLED CHICKEN WITH KACHUMBARETTE

You can use a mortar and pestle or buy a readymade variety from the supermarket.

SERVING

Serves: **2**

Every now and then my Indian spice taste buds are awakened. After all, I was raised eating hearty healthy Indian food until I started exploring other cuisines through my travels.

When I want an Indian curry, this simple spiced chicken with a tangy vinaigrette, inspired by the traditional *kachumbar* salad, pacifies my cravings. Kachumbar is a typical Indian salad made from sliced onion, fresh tomatoes, chillies, and white vinegar. My mom calls it Kachumbarette: a mixture of Kachumbar and vinaigrette. Chicken thighs work best with this recipe, but breasts are great too. Best accompanied with some cool yoghurt on the side.

INGREDIENTS

½ cup yoghurt

1 tablespoon olive oil

1 teaspoon ground coriander

½ teaspoon ground cumin

¾ teaspoon Kashmir chilli powder

½ teaspoon ground turmeric

¼ teaspoon ground garam masala

Pinch ground cardamom

1 teaspoon ginger and garlic paste

1 teaspoon dried fenugreek leaves *(kasuri methi)* (optional)

Salt

500 grams boneless chicken thighs or breasts, washed and cut into medium pieces

For the kachumbarettte

½ small onion, finely chopped

½ medium tomato, finely chopped

½ green chilli, finely chopped

1 tablespoon coriander leaves and stems, finely chopped

1 tablespoon white vinegar

1 tablespoon olive oil

Salt

Freshly ground black pepper

METHOD

1. Preheat the oven to 170°C.

2. In a large bowl, combine the yoghurt with the oil, coriander, cumin, chilli, turmeric, garam masala, cardamom, ginger and garlic paste, and dried fenugreek leaves. Season with salt.

3. Add the chicken pieces to the yoghurt marinade and mix well.

4. Transfer the chicken to a baking tray and place in the preheated oven. Bake for about 30 minutes or until the chicken is cooked and the marinade is browning slightly. Remove the tray from the oven and let the meat rest for at least 5 minutes before serving.

5. Making the kachumbarette: In a separate glass bowl, combine the onion, tomato, chilli, coriander, vinegar, and olive oil. Season with salt and pepper. Mix well. Drizzle the mixture over the chicken and serve with a side salad and yoghurt.

Do you know how to check if chicken is cooked?
Touch the meat with your finger; can you feel a slight bounce?

Or if you pierce the chicken with a fork or toothpick and it comes out effortlessly, it's done.

SKILL

LEMONGRASS-INFUSED INDIAN COCONUT STEW

INGREDIENTS

2 tablespoons coconut oil

4 green cardamom pods

2 cinnamon sticks

1 bay leaf

1 medium onion, finely sliced

4 green chillies, slit in half

1 tablespoon fresh ginger, finely sliced

500 grams boneless chicken thighs, washed and cut into medium pieces

½ cup chicken stock (using ½ stock cube)

3 (2-inch) lemongrass stems, bruised

1 cup coriander leaves with stems, finely chopped

1 cup coconut milk

Salt

Pinch sugar

1 tablespoon lime juice

Sometimes just that one ingredient or cooking technique is enough to whip up an old-time dish into something totally snazzy.

That is exactly what the aromatic flavours of lemongrass does for a popular South Indian chicken stew. It is served with steamed rice, *porotta* (Kerala's famous layered flatbread), or the classic appams (fermented rice bread made with rice batter and coconut milk).

Adding the lemongrass definitely gives this dish a whole new zesty taste-lift!

Make it 1 cup if you'd like to make this recipe as a soup.

SERVING

Serves: **2**

METHOD

1. Heat the oil in a pan on medium heat. Add the cardamom, cinnamon, and bay leaf and fry until aromatic. Then add the onion, green chillies, and ginger and sauté until the onion is translucent.

2. Next, add the chicken and sauté for 2 minutes or until the colour of the chicken changes to white. Add the chicken stock followed by the lemongrass and coriander. Allow to simmer on low heat for a few minutes.

3. Check if the chicken is cooked. Add the coconut milk. Season with salt and sugar. Continue to simmer for 5 minutes. Remove from the heat and finish with the lime juice. Remove the lemongrass and serve the stew with steamed rice.

You can remove the lemongrass just before serving.

SKILL

Do you know the best way to prepare lemongrass for cooking? Peel off the outer tough leaves, cut the bulb at the bottom, and using a rolling pin or back of a knife, gently whack the lemon grass. This releases the lemony flavour!

MOM'S KHEEMA PAV

INGREDIENTS

2 tablespoons
olive oil

1 medium onion,
finely chopped

2 green chillies,
finely chopped

6 or 7 curry leaves,
rinsed

1 medium tomato,
finely chopped

1-inch piece fresh
ginger, finely
chopped

2 garlic cloves,
finely chopped

250 grams
minced mutton
meat (medium
ground)

1 teaspoon salt

½ teaspoon
ground turmeric

½ teaspoon
freshly ground
black pepper

1 teaspoon
white vinegar

½ to 1 teaspoon
butter, at room
temperature

2 pav or dinner
rolls, cut in half

1 tablespoon fresh
coriander leaves,
washed and finely
chopped

Kheema pav, or minced meat with toast, is a common Mumbaikar (people who hail from Mumbai) snack or even a meal by itself.

Prepared with freshly ground pepper, powdered spices and coriander leaves, and served with pav bread (a small loaf originally introduced by the Portuguese), anyone familiar with this dish might start salivating at its very mention.

Minced Indian mutton is preferable, but lamb or beef work equally well. My recommendation would be to add peas and small pieces of chopped potato, while keeping the minced meat a little watery, so you can dip the bread pieces into the light, peppery gravy.

Worried about the spice aroma lingering around your kitchen? Not anymore. Burn an incense stick or use an essential oil diffuser to neutralize the air after you're done cooking.

SERVING

Serves: **2**

METHOD

1. Place a shallow frying pan on low heat and add the oil.

2. When the oil is slightly warm, add the onion, green chillies, and curry leaves.

3. Sauté until the onion turns translucent and almost lightly brown. Add the chopped tomato, ginger, and garlic, and continue to sauté for 2 more minutes. You can add a few splashes of water to ensure the mixture doesn't burn and stirs well.

4. Add the minced meat and stir well. The meat will begin to brown.

5. Add the salt, turmeric, and pepper. Stir well and add the vinegar. Stir one more time, cover the pan with a lid, and cook on medium heat.

6. After 5 minutes, remove the lid and allow the flavoured stock to completely evaporate, or remove the pan from the heat when the stock reaches your desired consistency.

7. Preparing the pav/dinner rolls: Put a griddle or a flat pan on medium heat. Apply the butter generously to the sliced open surfaces of the bread and place them buttered-side down on the hot griddle. Toast for a few minutes and turn over.

8. Garnish the *kheema* with coriander just before serving along with the toasted pav or dinner rolls.

AUNTY DIANA'S RED DAL

SERVING

Serves: **3 to 4**

INGREDIENTS

1 cup red lentils
(masoor dal)

1 teaspoon red
chilli powder

½ teaspoon
ground turmeric

1 medium onion,
finely chopped

Salt

1½ tablespoons
ghee

1 teaspoon
mustard seeds

2 garlic cloves,
crushed

½ teaspoon
asafoetida powder

135 grams
tomato paste

Lentil curries in India vary between the many states, from using different types of lentils, mixing them, thick to thin consistency, served with rotis (Indian flatbread), or a bowl of rice.

Whatever the form, lentil curry *(dal)* is my perfect comfort food. When all else fails, it's always dal and some hot steamed rice to the rescue.

This version was introduced to our family by my aunt Diana, who picked it up from an Emirati family who had their own take on the dish. With tomato paste as the base, this is a truly unique version, bright red and bursting with tomato tanginess balanced with tempered spices. Enough said.

METHOD

1. Rinse the lentils well, transfer to a pot with about 3 cups of water, and place over medium heat.

2. Add the red chilli powder, turmeric, and onion and season with salt. Let the lentils simmer for about 20 minutes or until they soften.

3. While the lentils are cooking, place another saucepan on medium heat and melt the ghee. When warm, add the mustard seeds and allow them to crackle. Add the garlic and fry until slightly golden brown. Add the asafoetida and then the tomato paste. Fry, stirring, until a smooth paste forms and you can see the ghee separating from the mixture.

4. Add the lentils to the tomato paste mixture and stir well. Add about ½ cup of lukewarm water for a lighter consistency, as preferred. Adjust the seasoning and bring to a boil once, to ensure that all the ingredients are well blended.

While preparing your dal, **think about what you would like to go along with it.** White rice? Then put a portion on to cook. Side salad? Then wash the leaves and leave them to dry right at the start and freshly prepare the salad toward the end.

Thinking about your plate helps you plan your steps in the kitchen so everything comes together.

EZRA'S EASY CHICKEN STIR FRY

SERVING

Serves: **2**

INGREDIENTS

2 boneless chicken breasts

Dash white vinegar

Salt

Freshly ground black pepper

Extra-virgin olive oil

1 medium onion, finely sliced

¼ each red and green bell peppers, sliced into batons (see Skill tip)

4 or 5 button mushrooms, sliced

1 medium tomato, finely sliced

½ teaspoon ground allspice or ground garam masala

My boss Ezra is my mother hen at work, forever feeding me all sorts of homemade yummies. From pancakes to pasta, Ezra packs a little something for me every now and then.

And once, when it was a really busy season and she knew I wasn't cooking much at home, she handed me this chicken stir-fry recipe. It was such a life saver. It's so simple and quick, this is my no-fail recipe any time.

I boil the chicken and cut the vegetables the night before, then in the morning all I need to do is sauté them together, drizzle with olive oil, and *c'est tout!* Thanks, Ezra!

METHOD

1. Preparing the chicken breast: In a small saucepan bring to boil enough water to cover the chicken breasts. Put in the chicken along with the vinegar; season with salt and pepper. Boil the chicken for 5 to 7 minutes or until the centre feels slightly firm. Turn the heat off and transfer the chicken breasts to a plate. Once cooled, with a sharp knife, slice the chicken diagonally into medium slices.

2. In a wide frying pan on medium-high heat, drizzle a little olive oil, and when slightly heated, add the onion, bell peppers, and mushrooms and sauté for a few minutes.

3. When the onions just turn translucent, add the tomato and sauté until it begins to soften.

4. Add the chicken slices to the pan along with the ground allspice or garam masala. Season with salt and pepper and continue to sauté for 5 minutes.

5. Remove the pan from the heat, drizzle with extra-virgin olive oil, and gently stir.

SKILL

Batons are **broad even thick strips** (or even sticks). They are usually 2 to 3 inches long and about ½ inch thick (something that's thicker and shorter than a French fry).

CHILLI PRAWNS IN LEMON AND GARLIC BUTTER

SERVING

Serves: **2**

INGREDIENTS

8 large, medium, or king prawns, peeled with tail on

2 pinches sea salt

Olive oil

4 garlic cloves, 1 peeled and crushed, 3 unpeeled and roughly crushed

1 teaspoon crushed red chilli flakes

Knob butter, divided

1 lemon, thinly sliced

Few flat-leaf parsley sprigs, finely chopped

Prawns prepared with the right sauces are heart-warmers after a long day's work. The combination of lemon, butter, garlic, chilli, olive oil, and fresh prawns in this dish is delectable and even more so when you dip some crusty bread into it.

This recipe is from my gal pal, Kanta, who is a queen bee at a global tech company. She kicks butts at her workplace but is also a true-blood foodie. We often survey the city for the latest eats and bites and over many a glass of vino enjoy long conversations about work, relationships, and life.

Each bite of this dish reminds me of the ten-day road trip we took from Madrid to Barcelona, enjoying pub crawls in Madrid, wine-tastings in Valdepenas, tapas in Barcelona, history walks through Toledo, and orange-laden trees in Valencia. Salut to that and *muchas gracias* for this recipe, Kanta!

METHOD

1. Run the tip of a sharp knife down the back of each prawn and remove the vein (deveining the prawn). Wash and drain the prawns. Marinate in the sea salt, a generous drizzle of olive oil, peeled garlic clove, and red chilli flakes.

2. In a small frying pan on medium heat, melt half the butter and lay the slices of lemon evenly on the bottom of the pan. Dot the remaining butter on top of the lemon slices. Add the 3 unpeeled and roughly crushed garlic cloves.

3. Once the butter begins to sizzle, place the prawns over the lemon slices. Cook for 1 to 2 minutes on each side or until firm.

4. To finish off, remove the pan from the heat and add the parsley leaves with a sprinkle of sea salt. Transfer the prawns to a plate, and drizzle with the lemon and garlic butter sauce. Serve immediately with warm crusty bread.

SASS!

This dish is a **winner for parties.** Plate the prawns with the lemon and garlic butter sauce in one of those brown ceramic dishes (just like tapas served in Spain). Bring out your best wine and pass around the warm bread.

WANNABE LEBANESE KOUSA

SERVING

12 meatballs,
for 2 to 3 people

My Lebanese friend Marguerite introduced this dish to me way back during undergrad days.

With the first bite, I knew I had to create a hack version because stuffing the courgettes was time-consuming.

Now I can savour this dish whenever I want, have it as a soup, or add more rice to it, and it's a meal on its own.

METHOD

1. Making the meatballs: in a bowl, combine all the ingredients and mix well. Shape the mixture into small meatballs and set aside.

2. Place a deep pot on medium heat. Add the water. As it begins to heat up, add the diced courgettes, tomato paste, garlic, and salt. Lower the heat and gently add the meatballs. Simmer for 30 to 40 minutes, until the sauce has reduced. Every now and then, gently shake the pot, holding the handles. Avoid using a spoon to stir so the meatballs don't break up.

3. Gently stir in the butter and olive oil. Remove the pan from the heat and serve the kousa with a dollop of fresh yoghurt.

INGREDIENTS

For the meatballs

2 tablespoons long grain rice, washed

250 to 270 grams lean minced beef

1 medium tomato, finely diced

½ onion, finely diced

⅓ cup flat-leaf parsley, finely chopped

Pinch chilli powder

1 teaspoon ground cinnamon

½ teaspoon freshly ground black pepper

1 teaspoon salt

For the courgette base

4 cups water

1 cup courgettes or baby marrows, cut into medium dice

2 heaped tablespoons tomato paste

1 garlic clove, crushed

1 teaspoon salt

1 teaspoon butter, at room temperature

2 tablespoons olive oil

Fresh yoghurt, for serving

SASS!

Usually when I cook dishes that have some **downtime**, I use the free moments for **meditation**.

Plug in my ear phones, swipe to my meditation app on my phone, sit back, close my eyes, and hit play.

SIMPLICIOUS EASY STEAK

SERVING

Serves: **1**

INGREDIENTS

1 rib eye steak, at least 1 inch thick and well marbled with fat

Sea salt

Freshly ground black pepper

1½ teaspoons butter

2 garlic cloves

1 rosemary sprig

'Hey, how do you make a good steak?' This is a question I get asked often.

I've come to realize that people associate steak with fine restaurants; however, you can make some pretty awesome steak at home. All you need is a good quality cut from your butcher, salt, freshly ground pepper, a sprig of rosemary, and a knob of butter.

Steak has so much flavour that you really don't need much to accompany it. I enjoy mine with a little bit of cool cucumber and yoghurt dressing with a hint of sumac (a Middle Eastern dried powder with a lemony flavour), a side salad, or some simple potato mash.

METHOD

1. Season the steak well with salt and pepper on both sides and set aside.

2. In a heavy skillet on medium heat, begin to melt the butter. Add the garlic cloves and rosemary. Once the butter starts to get aromatic, place the steak in the pan and raise the heat to high. Sear the steak for a minute on each side (it's important to keep the heat high as that 'seals' the meat and locks in the juices as well as giving it that delicious grilled taste).

3. Sprinkle some water into the skillet and let the water sizzle. Cover the skillet with a lid and lower the heat to medium. Continue to cook the steak, flipping it after a minute or so, spooning the flavoured butter over the steak.

4. Press firmly in the centre of the steak and, depending how you like it done, stop or continue to cook on medium heat. Steak is best eaten medium, i.e., when cut, the juices run clear. Take the skillet off the heat and season the steak with more pepper, if you like. Let the steak rest for 10 minutes.

5. Slice and serve with your favourite side dish.

SKILL

A chef once told me you can never overseason a steak, but **you can definitely underseason it.** So, don't feel shy—trust your senses and go for it.

WATERMELON AND FETA CHEESE SALAD

SERVING

Serves: **2**

INGREDIENTS

4 cups seedless watermelon cubes, chilled

1½ cups small cubes feta cheese

1 tablespoon extra-virgin olive oil

Leaves from a few fresh mint sprigs, chopped

1 lime, juice squeezed

Pinch salt

Pinch freshly ground black pepper

Handful chopped walnuts (optional)

It was the middle of summer and I was working as an intern at the beach club of a famous resort in Dubai.

While guests were "soaking in the sun" I was getting fried. While running up and down the beach trying to meet their endless demands, I couldn't help noticing the unending line of watermelon and feta cheese bowls being served out from the kitchen. They looked so refreshing and cool under the glaring sun.

And so, this salad is an ode to that not-so-fun intern experience, but what came out of it is here to stay. Now I can dig this sweet and salty flavourful salad all by myself. This dish can be prepared well ahead and chilled in the refrigerator.

Store the dressing separately and pour just before serving.

METHOD

1. Place the watermelon cubes in a large bowl. Add the feta cheese and gently mix.

2. In a small bowl, whisk together the olive oil, mint, lime juice, salt, and pepper.

3. Pour the dressing generously over the salad, and add the walnuts (if using). Gently mix with a spoon and serve immediately, chilled.

SASS!

This dish is **perfect as an after-meal** fruit snack or a side dish when you have friends over.

It's simple but still earns you brownie points for whipping up fun takes on dishes.

CABBAGE GYOZAS

SERVING

Makes:
7 to 8 gyozas

INGREDIENTS

Salt

200 grams
minced chicken

Freshly ground
black pepper

1 or 2 spring
onions, finely
chopped

1-inch fresh
ginger, finely
chopped

1 garlic clove,
finely chopped

1 small-sized
cabbage

Olive oil

A Japanese dish, gyozas are meat dumplings wrapped with a thin dough, steamed and then pan fried.

When I was doing the keto diet, my mom tested a 'keto-version' of a gyoza made with cabbage leaves. Now, whenever I have some leftover minced meat, cabbage gyozas it is! Though you may think the steps are time consuming, the whole preparation is done in thirty minutes.

You can also prepare them ahead and store in the fridge. They can be eaten either steamed or pan fried. Remember, the dipping sauce is where the magic lies!

METHOD

To prepare the gyozas

1. Season a large pot of water with ½ teaspoon of salt and put it on medium heat.

2. Put the minced chicken in a bowl and season with salt and pepper. Add the spring onion, ginger, and garlic. Mix well and set aside.

3. Choose 8 to 10 tender leaves from the cabbage. As the water comes to a boil, add the cabbage leaves. Cover the pot with a lid and turn the heat off. After 1 to 2 minutes, remove the leaves (keep the hot water in the pot as you'll need it later), and set them aside.

4. In the centre of one cabbage leaf, place a teaspoon of chicken filling. Fold in the sides first and then, starting from the bottom, roll the cabbage leaf over the filling and away from you, making sure it is fully enclosed. You can secure the roll with a toothpick.

5. Repeat step 4 to make the rest of the gyozas.

To cook the gyozas

1. Place a steamer insert into the same pot of hot water. Turn the heat on and as the water comes back to a boil, place the gyozas on the steamer, cover the pot with a lid, and allow the chicken to steam for about 10 minutes. Remove the gyozas and set aside.

2. Place a frying pan on medium heat and sprinkle some olive oil into the pan. When the oil is slightly heated, add the gyozas and toast on both sides until slightly crispy and brown.

Chilli peanut sauce dip recipe on page 147

This recipe can be followed using **readymade dim sum** wrappers, which you can find in the supermarket. You can also **make extra gyozas and store them in the freezer.**

When ready to cook, steam them and have them as is or go a step further and pan fry them.

FRIED RICE BUDDHA BOWL

SERVING

Serves: **1**

I take much pride in sharing this recipe with you. It's something I created on the fly and now it's here to stay.

If I feel like eating something Asian and I have some of my favourite red rice and mixed colour quinoa leftovers, then in just under ten minutes I can have a steaming hot bowl ready.

This recipe is bursting with colours, flavours, and nutrition—zen for our eyes, taste, and soul. Wondering if it may taste better with some chicken in it? Of course! Throw in some cooked chicken (chop it to a similar size to the veggies) and toss it in right after step 2, before seasoning.

Just looking at this bowl makes me happy. Make some and you'll know why: it's like eating a rainbow.

Boil ¼ cup of red rice with 1 tablespoon of mixed colour quinoa beforehand and strain.

INGREDIENTS

Olive oil

½ cup chopped bell pepper, any two colours

1 medium broccoli floret, with stem, chopped

¾ cup courgette, chopped

1 red chilli, finely chopped

½ cup button mushrooms, chopped

1 teaspoon chilli garlic paste

Soy sauce

½ cup cooked red rice with mixed colour quinoa

Handful purple cabbage, finely chopped

Salt

Freshly ground black pepper

2 spring onions, finely chopped

3 or 4 fresh coriander leaves, for garnish

SKILL

The key to success with this dish is the size you chop the vegetables. The more **even and similar in size,** the easier it is to get the vegetables to cook at the same rate. So chop them small to medium and they will cook at the same pace.

METHOD

1. Into a wok or a wide frying pan on high heat, drizzle just enough olive oil to make the wok shine. Keep the heat high throughout the cooking process to give the 'fried' and 'charred' taste to the dish.

2. Add the chopped bell peppers, broccoli, courgette, chilli, and mushrooms. Stir fry until the mushrooms soften and the courgette is slightly charred.

3. Stir in the chilli garlic paste and a few splashes of soy sauce and continue to stir fry.

4. Add the red rice and quinoa, and purple cabbage. Begin to gently press down as if you are flattening the rice onto the wok bottom. When you hear the rice begin to crackle, stir and check for seasoning. Adjust with salt and pepper if required.

5. Turn the heat off and stir in the spring onions. Serve hot, garnished with the coriander leaves.

THIS ONE
IS A KEEPER...

THIS ONE IS A KEEPER...

All through the book I've mentioned various dips, sauces and chutneys that add an extra special something. Try not to be tempted to skip 'em, they're well worth it and make a world of difference.

Dips and sauces are flavour bombs and can give your dish a complete facelift. All it takes is a mix-and-match of ingredients and a good stir! Here are some of my favourite that I always turn to and go beautifully with some of the recipes mentioned earlier.

Chutneys are a concoction of aromatic herbs and spices blended into a well-combined, slightly coarse paste. Here are two of my all-time favourites. I love them for their simplicity and versatility.

1.	SRIRACHA SOY DIP	147
2.	CHILLI PEANUT SAUCE	147
3.	DILL AND GARLIC DIP	147
4.	GREEN CORIANDER AND MINT CHUTNEY	148
5.	COCONUT CHUTNEY	149

SRIRACHA SOY DIP

See page 66

INGREDIENTS

1 tablespoon sriracha sauce

2 teaspoons soy sauce

½ teaspoon honey

METHOD

Combine the sriracha, soy sauce, honey, and the residual juices from the shrimp. Serve, and enjoy dipping your wrap with every bite.

CHILLI PEANUT SAUCE

See page 140

INGREDIENTS

1 teaspoon peanut butter

3 to 4 tablespoons sriracha sauce

1 teaspoon soy sauce

METHOD

In a small bowl, combine the peanut butter, sriracha, and soy sauce and stir until well combined.

DILL AND GARLIC DIP

See page 106

INGREDIENTS

2 garlic cloves, crushed

2 tablespoons fresh dill, finely chopped

4 tablespoons cream cheese, at room temperature

2 tablespoons cold water

METHOD

Mix the garlic, dill, cream cheese, and water together until smooth and creamy in texture.

Dill &
garlic
dip

GREEN CORIANDER
AND MINT CHUTNEY

INGREDIENTS

1 cup fresh coriander leaves, rinsed

½ cup mint leaves, rinsed

1 or 2 green chillies, or as preferred

1-inch piece fresh ginger

1 teaspoon cumin seeds

2 garlic cloves, peeled

1 tablespoon lime juice

Salt

METHOD

Combine all the ingredients in a blender. Add a little water to help initiate the blending. The consistency must be slightly thick, so check occasionally and add water as needed.

Transfer the contents to a bowl and adjust the seasoning, if required.

chilli peanut sauce

COCONUT CHUTNEY

INGREDIENTS

½ cup fresh coconut, grated

1 green chilli

½ tablespoon Bengal gram

¼-inch fresh ginger

Salt

1 tablespoon coconut oil

¼ teaspoon mustard seeds

4 or 5 curry leaves

1 dried red chilli, broken, optional

METHOD

1. Combine the coconut, green chilli, Bengal gram, and ginger in a blender. Season with salt and add a little water to help initiate the blending. The consistency must be slightly thick, so check occasionally and add water as needed. Transfer the contents to a bowl and adjust the seasoning, if required.

2. Next, heat the coconut oil in a small, deep frying pan on medium heat. When heated, add the mustard seeds. Once they have crackled, add the curry leaves and red chilli (if using). Stir for a few seconds and immediately pour the mixture over the coconut chutney. Stir well and serve at room temperature.

SWEET
ENDINGS

1.	EASY TIRAMISU	**154**
2.	MOLTEN CHOCOLATE CAKE IN A MUG	**156**
3.	BANANA MUG CAKE	**157**
4.	BISCUIT PUDDING	**160**
5.	PANEER KHEER	**161**
6.	'SOKY' HOT CHOCOLATE	**162**
7.	BERRY'D BREAD LOVE POTS	**164**
8.	NO NAUGHTY NUTTY GOLDEN MYLK	**166**

SWEET ENDINGS

Girlfriend, what's a day without some sugar-high in it?

Now I certainly don't fall into the category of the girl who hides her sugar cravings in a closet. In fact, I unabashedly shout out, 'Embrace that sweet tooth!' I've come to realise sweet endings don't have to be loaded with sugar and cream. Many combinations of superfoods and healthy ingredients taste just as good, if not better.

And so, here are the sweet endings I turn to on the days I feel that after-dinner craving.

These are simple, straightforward, no fuss, and almost guilt-free because I keep the portion size small and use various fun ingredients to keep the kitchen goddess mojo going.

EASY TIRAMISU

SERVING

2 (0.5-L) medium mason jars

INGREDIENTS

½ cup
whipping cream

2 to 3 tablespoons
sugar, or to taste

½ teaspoon
vanilla essence

250 grams
mascarpone cheese

2 teaspoons
instant coffee powder (or more if you like a caffeine kick)

2 tablespoons
apple juice or 2 tablespoons Kahlua (coffee liqueur)

100ml cold water

8 to 9 ladyfinger sponges

Unsweetened cocoa powder, for dusting

I make really good tiramisu, or at least that's what I was told growing up serving tiramisu at most of our house parties.

I love the flavours of coffee-soaked ladyfinger sponges and sweetened mascarpone cheese combined in one bite. This recipe was probably my first experiment with desserts as a little girl.

I make this version in a mason jar that I keep to set in the refrigerator for the next day. It's something to look forward to on my drive home after a long day at the office, or if I have a friend coming round for coffee and a chat, it's nice to whip this out as an extra treat.

SKILL

The secret to a good tiramisu is the taste **proportion of coffee-soaked sponge to whipped sweet cheese-cream.** So, make sure the coffee concoction is strong and the cheese-cream mixture is slightly sweet. The combination is bliss.

METHOD

1. Bring all the ingredients, except the water, to room temperature.

2. In a large bowl, use a hand beater to whip the cream, sugar, and vanilla until the mixture turns to a light and fluffy foam. Fold in the mascarpone cheese to the mixture and set aside.

3. In a medium bowl, mix the coffee and apple juice or Khalua with the cold water.

4. Begin the layering: Spread a tablespoon of the cheese-cream mixture at the bottom of the mason jar. Next, working with one ladyfinger sponge at a time, dip it quickly in and out of the cold coffee concoction and lay over the cheese-cream mixture in the mason jar. Dip as many as required to cover the base.

5. Use the back of a tablespoon to spread some cheese-cream mixture evenly over the ladyfingers. Repeat step 4 to create more layers of coffee-dipped ladyfingers covered with cheese-cream mixture, making sure you finish with a top layer of cheese-cream.

6. Cover and refrigerate for at least 2 hours. Dust the top with cocoa powder right before serving.

MOLTEN CHOCOLATE CAKE IN A MUG

SERVING

Serves: **1**

INGREDIENTS

2 tablespoons
70% dark chocolate, chopped into small pieces, plus 1 square

1 tablespoon
unsalted butter, chopped into small pieces, plus more for brushing the mug

1 egg

2 tablespoons
sugar

Dash vanilla essence

2 tablespoons
all-purpose flour, passed through a small sieve

Pinch baking powder

Sprinkle salt

Vanilla ice cream, optional, for serving

The first time I tried this was during my internship as a student chef.

I still remember how wide eyed I went when I first pierced my fork into the cake and saw that perfectly melted chocolate centre ooze out.

Here's my version of creating the same effect at home. Mug cakes like these don't need a reason for you to indulge. The rest can wait, but first . . . Cake!

METHOD

1. Preheat the oven to 180°C.

2. Place 2 tablespoons of chopped chocolate and the butter in a glass bowl and microwave for 45 seconds. Remove the bowl at regular intervals, and with a wooden spoon stir until the chocolate and butter are completely melted and smooth. Set aside.

3. In a medium-sized bowl, using a hand beater whisk the egg, sugar, and vanilla essence until pale yellow, creamy, and slightly frothy.

4. Fold the cooled down butter-chocolate mix into the whisked eggs.

5. Fold in the flour, baking powder, and salt. Stir thoroughly until well combined and no flour lumps are seen.

6. Dip the chocolate square right into the centre of the mug before placing the mug in the preheated oven. Bake for 15 minutes. Remove and let the mug rest for 2 minutes. Serve warm with a scoop of vanilla ice cream, if preferred.

SASS!

Mug cakes are **great for surprise visitors.** Also, to play with flavours, you can always swap the chocolate square for peanut butter, shredded coconut, or muddled berries.

BANANA MUG CAKE

SERVING

Serves: **1**

INGREDIENTS

Small knob butter, at room temperature, plus **1 tablespoon**, melted

1 egg

2 tablespoons honey

½ ripe or frozen banana, mashed

2 tablespoons milk

1 tablespoon walnuts, chopped

1 teaspoon chia seeds

Pinch ground cinnamon

Dash vanilla essence

4 tablespoons all-purpose flour

½ teaspoon baking powder

The aroma of honey-caramelised banana, spicy cinnamon, and toasted walnuts wafting through the air is instantly therapeutic to my senses.

On a day when nothing goes as planned—I've goofed up on a simple task at work, and I've chewed off my manicure while listening to my friend talk about her latest tiff with hubby—I can whip up this banana mug cake, sit back, let out a loud unapologetic sigh, and with the first bite know that everything is going to be A-okay.

Can something so perfect be contained in a mug? Well, this kick-ass recipe definitely can. Over to you!

METHOD

1. Preheat the oven to 180°C.

2. Using your fingers, grease a wide-bottomed tall mug with the room-temperature butter.

3. In a bowl, using a hand beater, whip the egg, honey, melted butter, mashed banana, and milk until you have a smooth runny batter.

4. Next, stir in the chopped walnuts, chia seeds, cinnamon, and vanilla.

5. Pass the flour and baking powder through a sieve over the bowl. Using a wooden spoon, gently fold in the flour mixture until it is well mixed and no flour is visible.

6. Pour the mixture directly into the mug and place the mug in the oven. Bake for 25 to 30 minutes or until a toothpick inserted into the centre of the cake comes out clean.

SKILL

What does it mean to **'fold' flour** into a batter?

Folding is a technique that **traps air into the batter.** Best done with a wooden spoon or rubber spatula, the action is almost like swirling the spoon around the edges of the mug (or bowl) in one direction. It's almost like wrapping the batter over and over. Whichever direction you pick, **stick to it** until all the flour is folded in. Switching directions will release the air you've worked so hard to trap in.

BISCUIT PUDDING

SERVING

Makes:
One 4.5-inch square dish

INGREDIENTS

1 (160-gram) tin cream

3 tablespoons chocolate drink powder mix

½ teaspoon unsweetened cocoa powder

3 tablespoons sugar

1 tablespoon milk, or more, for mixing

100 grams Marie biscuits or plain butter biscuits

Handful pistachios, chopped

My brother introduced this recipe to our family. He learnt it from a gym buddy (while some push for bicep curl reps, my brother pushes for pudding recipes).

The simplicity of the pudding belies how addictive it is. This dessert needs some time to set, so I often make a bowl and set it in the fridge for the next day.

One of my favourite evening wind-down routines is a cup of Nespresso (did I mention I'm a caffeine addict?), a small portion of biscuit pudding, and a movie.

I'm a happy bunny!

METHOD

1. In a bowl, mix the cream, chocolate powder, cocoa powder, and sugar, adding enough milk as necessary to achieve a smooth consistency.

2. Spoon a little bit of the chocolate-cream mixture into the bottom of the dish, followed by a layer of biscuits. Continue creating layers, making sure the final layer is chocolate-cream.

3. Top with the chopped pistachio nuts and place the dish in the fridge to set for at least 2 hours. Serve cold or at room temperature.

SKILL

Make sure the cream layers are thicker than the biscuits. Avoid creating double layers of biscuits in panic if you see the biscuits sink into the cream. Once the pudding sets, cut into it like a regular cake.

PANEER KHEER

SERVING

Serves: **2**

INGREDIENTS

2 cups milk

2 to 3 tablespoons sugar

3 tablespoons almonds, crushed

½ teaspoon ground cardamom

½ cup paneer, crumbled

A few strands saffron, soaked in **1 tablespoon** lukewarm milk

Paneer, or cottage cheese, is India's most popular cheese variant and is extremely versatile for use in both savoury and sweet dishes.

The light, spongy, rich, and creamy flavour blends so well with various ingredients that it's almost the 'meat of choice' for vegetarians. I especially like this sweetened version of paneer because not only is it simple, it's great for using up any leftover paneer, plus I've just packed some protein into my dessert.

How's that for ending your day on a sweet and nutritionally high note?

METHOD

1. Place a saucepan on medium heat and pour the milk into it. Bring it to a boil.

2. Add the sugar, almonds, and cardamom to the milk and let it boil for about 10 minutes.

3. Add the paneer and simmer for 5 minutes. Remove from the heat and stir in the soaked saffron milk. Serve warm.

SKILL

When reheating in a microwave, always make sure you use a **microwave-friendly container;** glass or ceramic is best.

'SOXY' HOT CHOCOLATE

SERVING

Serves: 1

INGREDIENTS

1 cup milk

1 tablespoon cocoa powder

¼ cup 70% dark chocolate

Dash vanilla essence

1 big scoop vanilla ice cream

Ground cinnamon, for dusting

As my friend and I walked out of a blockbuster Bollywood movie, she asked me what I thought of the male actor.

She caught me by surprise because I was at that exact moment daydreaming about how sexy and hot he looked on screen. I blurted out "He was just too soxy!" Lol. Well, I had wanted to say he was sexy and hot. The combination word is now an inside joke adjective in my friend circle.

There's no better way to describe this hot chocolate than as the ultimate homemade hot chocolate I've ever had. Cuddled on a couch, dim lights, some blues playing in the background, and this soxy cuppa is my kinda late evening.

METHOD

1. Pour the milk into a saucepan on medium heat and stir in the cocoa powder.

2. As the milk is just about to boil, take the pan off the heat, stir in the dark chocolate until melted and add the vanilla essence.

3. Pour the hot chocolate into a mug, then scoop the ice cream gently on top and dust with cinnamon.

SASS!

As I sip on hot chocolate, I use times like these to **reflect on my day**—which moments made me light up and which ones not so much. In a way, it's making each sip intentional as I gear up for the next day.

BERRY'D BREAD LOVE POTS

SERVING

4 (13-cl) mini mason jars

INGREDIENTS

Handful mixed pecans and almonds, chopped

2 to 2½ tablespoons butter

3 white bread slices, crusts removed

170 grams evaporated milk

90 grams condensed milk

2 or 3 drops vanilla essence

Pinch ground cinnamon

½ cup mixed berries, muddled

I really enjoy developing recipes from scratch. My mom and I often bounce recipe ideas and ingredient combinations off each other, which lead us straight into the kitchen.

You don't always get the recipes right on the first try, but that's the fun in it: to keep tweaking as you go. There is much joy in relying on your taste buds, experiences, and flavours or experimenting with exotic ingredients you've found at the supermarket.

This is one such fun recipe that was weekend cooking therapy; it's like berry cheesecake and French toast come together layered in mini pots.

Whether you're holding one for yourself or handing them out at a party, this dessert spreads love in cute little pots.

SASS!

This is a perfect dessert to **make a day ahead** if you're calling friends or family over. It can be served cold, at room temperature, or warm, which makes it super versatile.

The jars store well and in fact always taste better the next day as the bread soaks up the sweet, berry and nutty flavours.

METHOD

1. Put a small frying pan on low heat. Add the nuts to the pan and dry roast them until slightly brown and fragrant. Set aside to cool.

2. Put a large frying pan on low heat. The pan needs to be big enough to hold the bread slices. Put the butter in the pan and once melted, add the bread slices and toast until golden brown. Remove from the heat and cut the bread into mini squares.

3. While the bread is toasting, place a saucepan on low heat and combine the evaporated milk, condensed milk, vanilla, and cinnamon in the pan. Heat just enough to warm the milk but not boil it. Remove from the heat and set aside.

4. In a mason jar, layer the ingredients, starting with the muddled berries followed by a few tablespoons of the milk mix, a few toasted bread squares, and another few tablespoons of the milk mix—just enough to soak into the bread. Finish by sprinkling a few roasted nuts on top. Seal and refrigerate for at least 1 hour.

5. Repeat until all the mason jars have been layered and garnished with nuts.

NO NAUGHTY NUTTY GOLDEN MYLK

SERVING

Serves: **2**

INGREDIENTS

½ cup
cashew nuts

4 dates, pitted
(seeds removed)

Few strands
saffron

1 cup cold water

1 teaspoon
ground turmeric

2 teaspoons
ground cardamom

Naturally sweet, satisfying and guilt-free; all I need to do is blitz—hurray!

Beverages like these are perfect for days when the only activity I'm willing to do is turn the blender switch on and off. Also, when I feel I need to cut back on sugar, or maybe just want a glass of cold milk, this mylk version (the hipster term for nondairy milks) is perfect.

Cheating without guilt is what this dessert is all about. Slurp!

METHOD

1. Soak the cashew nuts, dates, and saffron in the water for at least 20 minutes.

2. In a blender, pour in the soaked cashew nuts, saffron, and dates along with the water. Add the turmeric and cardamom. Blend until completely combined and smooth.

Add a few ice cubes to enjoy on a hot summer's day.

 SASS!

Since we're on all things turmeric, how about I share my **all-time favourite bedtime face mask?** I usually keep this on while I sip my golden mylk. Now I'm glowing inside and out!

2 tablespoons regular oatmeal
Pinch turmeric
1 teaspoon yoghurt
½ teaspoon honey
½ lime, juice squeezed

1. In a glass bowl, use your fingers to crush the oatmeal so it 'grinds' into coarse granules.

2. Add the turmeric, yoghurt, honey, and lime juice and mix well.

3. Apply the mask evenly to a cleansed and dried face. Leave the mask on for 15 minutes or until dry, then wash off with cold water. Tone and moisturize right after!

HOST YOUR PARTY
LIKE A PRO

—

SHE RULES OVER THE KITCHEN LIKE THE QUEEN SHE IS AND LIVES HAPPILY EVER AFTER.

—

HOST YOUR PARTY LIKE A PRO

I love feeding and entertaining my loved ones. There's something about cooking for family and friends that is so incredibly rewarding; it's like being able to give them a present handmade with love. And it can be as easy as grabbing a friend, some freshly brewed coffee, and a dessert mug bake.

But sometimes there's cause for a special occasion, like hosting a friend's 30th or celebrating a big life milestone, or even just bringing in the weekend with a cheer! To some, playing host can be all nerves. Guess what? Hosting a fancy party doesn't mean stressful and complicated! Here are my tips to help you when prepping for those special events when you want to go fancy and need to look all pro, uber-cool, and super relaxed.

"I've received your dinner invitation. It's like an invite from the queen! Do we need to wear evening gowns and our finest diamonds, because you've certainly made it sound like it?" And with that, my girlfriends and I crack up hard over the phone. Actually yes, I do make an effort with my invites, and it's not the first time I've heard guests say that I make it sound all fancy.

Now I'm going to let you in on my secret.

Breathe in and breathe out, here goes: Because I receive so many nudges and nags from friends and families looking for an invitation to a meal, I can't invest a lot of time in the kitchen whipping up dishes that are . . . "reputation friendly". I've got to keep my chin high, chest out, smile wide, and try not to pass out from exhaustion halfway through dinner (which, by the way, did happen once, but I have awesome friends who let me snore away to glory while they cleaned up). As a result, I devised a rather cool way to set the tone and mood for dinners that eased the pressure on me to make so many dishes. I put my plan into practice, and at the next dinner showed my friends who's queen of her kitchen.

1. DESIGN THE INVITATION

This is where it all begins—the invitation you send out. I usually design something really fun, and these days, there are plenty of apps to help you do that.

It sets the tone for the meal and gets people more excited about the event than a plain text WhatsApp, phone call, or email.

So, whether the meal is to celebrate the festive season, have casual fun with the girls, or woo that special somebody, sending out an invitation that's taken a bit of effort shows you're invested and excited about hosting them and that there's some serious culinary business coming up!

2. PLAN THE MENU

**Menu planning is key, especially if you're
hosting the meal by yourself.**

You need to add time for last-minute heating,
plating, and garnishes. You also need to socialize
and not act like a headless chicken dashing
between conversations and the kitchen.
And, the kitchen needs to look tidy and you
need to look your best.

So, girlfriend, pay heed because the following
tips have been tried and tested by yours truly.

- Dishes that can be prepared ahead of time are great choices because they knock one thing off the D-Day list.

- Keep a balance between cooking methods, as you won't want all the courses to be baked or sautéed. For example, you can have the starters baking in the oven while you prep the main course over the stove.

- My golden rule is to have self-serve starters, such as finger food, which buys you time for last-minute finishes and garnishing your hero main courses. Choose desserts that can be prepared a day ahead, which are great to wind down with while enjoying after-dinner conversations.

- Lastly, always ensure you ask your guests well beforehand about any allergies, dietary restrictions, new diets they may be on, and wish lists. Incorporating these in your menu means you went the extra mile to make them feel welcome.

3. SET THE TABLE

Woo your guests as they take their first steps towards the table.

The setting says it all. It's so true; even before we've tasted something, the way it's presented can get us salivating. And, of course, I take advantage of this. Here's how:

- Use a crisp tablecloth and lay a table runner on top in a colour that complements the colour of the tablecloth.

- Place dishes at different heights to give a layered effect. Use steel or wooden racks to set the main dish in the centre, or elevate the side dishes on either side of the table.

- Set a dinner plate directly in front of each dining chair. If salad or soup is being served, place a bowl on top of the dinner plate.

- Place the fork to the left of the dinner plate and the knife to the right of the dinner plate. Finally, set the spoon to the right of the knife.

- The water glass goes in the top right corner of the place setting, just above the knife.

- Finally, place the napkin either on the plate or underneath the fork.

4. CREATE THE AMBIANCE

- Mood lighting is amazing, not just to set the right atmosphere but also because low light is the perfect way to avoid your guests peering into the teeny-weeny details of what they're eating. Jokes apart, use candles, warm LED string lights, and yellow lamps to create a cosy and inviting atmosphere.

- Playing light background jazz or a chill music playlist does wonders and helps dilute any awkward silences. You could even keep your playlist accessible for your guests to choose their tunes, or even invite them to hook up their phone and share their favourite music. Music makes great conversation starters too!

- Ensure you've taken care of the smokers! If you have a balcony, place some ashtrays in strategic positions. If you don't have an outdoor space and you don't want anyone smoking inside, politely let your guests know your smoking policy well in advance, to avoid any uncomfortable discussions.

5. PUTTING IT ALL TOGETHER WILL LOOK SOMETHING LIKE THIS:

Three weeks before

- Think about your guest list and the occasion, whether it is a girlfriends' catch-up night, new friends you'd like to get to know better, relatives who just can't seem to get enough of you, or that special someone you want to impress.

- Check for everyone's availability.

- Design and send out e-invitations.

One week before

- Check back with your guests for confirmations and dietary restrictions, if any.

- Begin to plan your menu, keeping the menu-planning tips and your guests' dietary restrictions in mind.

- Once the menu is planned, think about how you would like the dishes to be plated and served. You can look at Pinterest for inspiration. Check to see if you have the serving dishes in store that you want, or whether you need to go shopping for something new.

- Pick up some pot pourri, scented candles, and additional warm LED lights, if you need more.

Two to three days before

- Visit the supermarket and shop for all the ingredients.

- Fill up the ice tray.

- Prepare your music playlist and test the speakers.

- Rearrange the seating in your living room, if necessary.

- Prepare any dishes that can be made well ahead of time and store well in the freezer or fridge.

- Assess your fridge and ensure you have enough space, if needed. Try and finish your leftovers (pack them for lunch or use them to make new dinners).

A day before

● Prepare any dishes that can be made a day in advance.

● Set up the tablecloth and place the candles. Set the table with plates, glasses, and cutlery—all face down.

● Make sure your home is sparkling clean, especially the restrooms. Put out a bowl of potpourri, a lovely scented handwash, and plenty of hand towels.

● If you're using flowers to perk up the place, arrange them in a vase and place them where you need them to add that natural touch.

● Place ashtrays on the balcony.

● Make sure the trash has been emptied and that you have a bigger trash container provisioned for the evening.

● Prepare a bar with glasses (overturned) and an empty water pitcher and ice bucket.

● Clean your kitchen counters on which you'll be working the next day.

Four to five hours before on the day

● Prepare your mise-en-place, which means setting out all the ingredients, including garnishes, you'll need to finish your dishes. Place them in order of use in one area of your working space.

● Set out a cutting board, tasting spoons, and knives. A hand cloth within reach is always handy too.

● Finalise the table setting by turning the plates, glasses, and cutlery face up.

Two hours before

● Place all the food (except dessert if it is chilled) on the counter.

● Prepare any finishing touches for the dishes.

● For finger foods, place them on serving dishes and on the living room centre table.

● For the bar, turn the glasses over, fill the water pitcher and ice bucket, and stock the beverages.

An hour before

● Light the candles.

● Start the playlist.

● Get dolled up. Don't forget the mascara!

● Eat a little something in case you forget to grab a bite in the midst of welcoming your guests and conversations.

● Drink a glass of water, relax, breathe, and tell yourself you're going to rock the evening!

It's magical how food brings people together, creates the heartiest laughter and etches the best memories.

RECIPES WHEN YOU ARE...

**Here are my top picks to pep, get you moving, or sorted.
You've got this.**

LOOKING TO USE LEFTOVERS

🥓	Bacon and Veggie Omelette On-the-Go	46
🍗	Chicken Kathi Rolls	68
🍗	Ezra's Easy Chicken Stir Fry	131
🥪	Bombay Sandwich	110
🍌	Banana Mug Cake	157

IN A HURRY

🧀	Grilled Cheese & PBJ Sandwich	42
🍎	Apple Cinnamon Oats in Five	48
🍚	Fried Rice Buddha Bowl	142
🍉	Watermelon and Feta Cheese Salad	138
🥛	Paneer Kheer	161

FEELING BLUE

🥣	Himalayan Porridge Bowl	57
🥦	Easy-Peasy Broccoli Soup	80
🫓	Shakkar Roti	102
🥒	Wannabe Lebanese Kousa	134
🍫	'Soxy' Hot Chocolate	162

INVITING PEOPLE OVER

- Pina Colada Quinoa Fruit Salad — 56
- Roasted Sweet Potato, Pine Nuts, and Kale Salad with Orange Honey Dressing — 86
- Chilli Prawns in Lemon and Garlic Butter — 132
- Pan con Tomate — 98
- Berry'd Bread Love Pots — 164

IN FOR SOME HEALTHY TLC

- Green Mung Bean Crêpes — 52
- Spicy Sriracha Prawn Wrap — 66
- Reej's Almond Bread — 96
- Cabbage Gyozas — 140
- No Naughty Nutty Golden Mylk — 166

ASKING FRIENDS TO STAY FOR A MEAL

- Savoury Flattened Rice (Poha) — 54
- Coconut Rice with Sautéed Green Chutney Vegetables — 84
- Bacon-Wrapped Goat's Cheese–Stuffed Dates — 104
- Indian Grilled Chicken with Kachumbarette — 124
- Molten Chocolate Cake in a Mug — 156

—

THE INGREDIENTS TO SUCCESS IN ANYTHING IN LIFE ARE GRATITUDE, EFFORT, AND LOVE.

—

ACKNOWLEDGEMENTS

Thank you . . .

God. For your providence in opening the doors, in your perfect timing that paved the way to make my dream of publishing a cookbook come true. I pray this book bears much fruit for all who collaborated with me on this journey and for those who will experience the book.

Mom. I don't think this book could ever have been done without you! I can't thank you enough for raising me to be the person that I am. Thank you for all your help testing and retesting the recipes and motivating me when I couldn't see the light at the end of the tunnel in this journey. You taught me how to seek freedom within boundaries and that going against the tide was perfectly fine.

Acha. You allowed me to dream with my eyes wide open and that I could be anything I wanted to be. Thank you for your advice even when I thought I never needed it, for being there when I thought I could handle things alone, and for letting the kid in me be alive. You've been my most honest critic and my biggest supporter in every project.

Viki, my older brother. I always wanted to grow up like you: self-driven, fearless, a go-getter. Your 'it's nice but you can do better' expression every time I made you try something new in the kitchen only made me do better. You've always been my silent supporter, and I know you've got my back through it all.

Deepti, my sis-in-law. For quickly growing accustomed to my shenanigans and for that smiling nod of approval each and every time I ventured in for something new and different. For your all-in, ever-patient, helpful attitude during the food photography.

Tittu (Kevin), my cousin brother. You are the best food critic I've met so far and it's bugging how you win every time we place a bet on anything to do with food and culture. You've been cheering me on all these years and somewhere I know you live through what I do. For your patience in reviewing my recipes word to word was so humbling and I'm so grateful.

Mable. You will always be like a second mom to me. For all the years we spent in the kitchen experimenting with recipes and talking about cooking techniques at length. For teaching me cooking is all about senses and instincts and goes beyond just memorising a recipe.

Ajish, my buddy. For continually urging me to send out the book proposal one more time and to never give up on my dream. For being my best travel buddy and for believing in me, more than I do in myself.

Svati, Nisha, and Pooja, my school girlfriends. From our grey-and-blue uniforms to now managing families of your own, I'm so proud of you all. Each of you has been so supportive and always encouraged me to follow my dreams. Thank you for filling my memory piggy bank with some of the best moments in my life.

Neha, my crazy girlfriend. Babe, you deserve special mention and you know why. I love the fact that when we go out for dinners we're unapologetically silent because our faces are stuffed, and that's okay for us. Thank you for giving me the loudest cheer always and for keeping a check so keenly on the book's progress.

Aji, Marguerite, Sarah, and Rohika, my friends from undergrad.
For all the memories we created together, for the kitchen disasters
and the restaurant slip-ups we now laugh over. I'm grateful you're
in my life, and I thank you for your friendship all these years.

Reeja. Even though we're more than a generation apart, we have
so much in common over mindless and fun banters about all
things food and lifestyle. Can't thank you and your family enough
for opening up your designer-like home for the photography and
for your amazing help to make me look glam for the pages.

 Kanta, Shami, Rahul, and Pooja, my precious friends. Without
you guys, this book wouldn't have been possible. To understand
the countless social occasions I had to turn down, the times I went
into a hole to meet my deadlines, for being my sounding board
about this book, and for keeping me sane through the process.

Shashank and Varun. You guys taught me that to achieve
something great, I needed to first get out of the rat race. For the
countless ideation sessions that got me comfortable to think out-
of-the-box while developing this book.

 To Swetha and Dev. The 'sweatyninjas' duo came into my life
at a time when I needed self-care and discipline the most. Your
regime to fitness and food helped me focus on the book and also
know you can achieve anything if you just put your mind to it.

 **To the Emirates Academy of Hospitality Management and the
Jumeirah Group.** For opening my world to the science of culinary
arts and world-class hospitality management.

To the entire team and partners at Mojo Advertising Dubai. The
place where I learnt the art of communication, the importance of
storytelling, and that the magic always lies in the details.

Andrea from Not on Saturday for the first illustration of my book while it was still at inception. You brought visuals to my words and for the first time sparked my excitement of what the completed book would look like.

To my work colleagues Ezra, Heba, Bilal, Kamran, Arshad, Ali, Lina, and Saeed. For making work so much fun, for being enthusiastic about the book, and for encouraging me on.

 Dimple and Uppi from Gone Fishing Cottages. You showed me that dishes prepared with love will always be that secret ingredient to great-tasting, finger-licking food.

 To Barry Morgan and Henriett Braun. Working with you guys is a dream come true and is more than I could have ever asked for my first book. I will always be indebted and grateful to you for holding this project close to your hearts and treating it no differently than I would. You guys are pure magic, and I hope through this book the world will see your talent.

 To my contributors. I trusted God and the universe to help support the funding of my project, and that's when you came in. Thank you to Reeja Eapen, Kanta Mirchandani, Geeta Jadhav, Anand Ashar, Surbhi Bhatia, Nisha Wagh, Joseph Thomas, Ajish Nair, Eldose Babu, Seema Vimal, Omer Khan, Asha Madhukar, Pooja and Rahul Parekh, Liju & Betsy Mathew, Sarah Shaw, Denzyl Gonsalves, and Rajesh Verma for believing in this book and for your contribution. It's people like you who make the world a happier place to live in.

 And last but not least, my publishers, The Dreamwork Collective. When I almost gave up on the dream of publishing, your email requesting our first meeting was God-sent. Kira, thank you for setting up an entity like The Dreamwork Collective that allows so many individuals to collaborate all for one reason: to do their dreamwork. Your kind and gentle approach is soul-warming;

thank you for taking me on board as a first-time author. Thalia, you are a dream editor. You've been patiently hand-holding me through the writing stages and edits to ensure we come up with a book we're all proud of. To Myriam for designing stunning visuals that bring my words to life, and to Meredith for ensuring all my commas, semi-colons, measurements, and instructions read well.

And finally, to the city of Dubai and its people. I've seen the city grow leaps and bounds. While for the world it's the centre of the most exciting attractions, for me it will always be the place where I spent my childhood years, learnt to love, faced failures, experienced personal breakthroughs, honed my skills, created lasting friendships, and now, published my first book.